MOUL...

THE TRUE STORY

Joel Neto

MOURINHO
THE TRUE STORY

Joel Neto

First published as *José Mourinho: O Vencedor*
in 2004 by Dom Quixote, Lisbon.
This English language edition published in 2005 by
First Stone Publishing,
an imprint of Corpus Publishing Limited
PO Box 8, Lydney,
Gloucestershire, GL15 6YD.

*The author would like to thank the following people for
their invaluable help: Estela Viegas, Francisco José Viegas,
José João Mendes Matos, Pedro Calhau,
Sara Fazendeiro and John Sellers.*

ISBN 1 904439 53 5

10 9 8 7 6 5 4 3 2 1

*Cover photograph: The Press Association.
Back cover photograph: José Mourinho and his sister Téresa
at the Sétubal sailing club in 1968.*

Contents

FOREWORD

A week before this book was published in Portugal, author Joel Neto, a leading Portuguese journalist, answered the phone in his holiday apartment in the Azores after a relaxing day on the beach. The caller was José Mourinho.

And for some 38 minutes of the 40-minute "conversation" that followed, Neto was subjected to ranting, accusations and threats from the man nicknamed "the gunfighter" because of his ability to keep his cool under pressure.

It gave Neto a first-hand insight into the contradictions that make up the remarkable mind of José Mourinho – Zé Mário to his family – a football coach *extraordinaire*, revered in Portugal. And although it would be fair to say the British press were sceptical when the man from Sétubal first arrived at Chelsea, it was in fact the beginning of a love affair with the media, which has made Mourinho the most written-about and photographed figure in British football.

Joel Neto and the rest of the Portuguese press had long known all about Mourinho's star quality. It was this that prompted the editor of *Grande Reportagem*, the Saturday supplement for which Neto works, to commission the longest profile feature in its history, in February 2004.

Denied an interview with Mourinho by the press office at FC Porto, the club he was coaching towards an astonishing victory in the Champions League, Neto began to research his article painstakingly by other means.

For the next two months he interviewed Mourinho's family, friends and colleagues past and present, some who loved him and others who patently did not. He put Mourinho under the microscope in a way that no one else has before or since.

The result was a sensational feature that appeared before Mourinho's adoring public in May last year. Neto had already had two novels and a war diary published in Portugal, and a smart editor at theindependent Lisbon publisher *Dom Quixote* was quick to spot the glint of gold in his latest work. Within days he was commissioned to turn his profile into a book.

It was published two months ahead of an "official" biography written by Mourinho's lifelong friend Luís Lourenço, which was to attract much comment and interest – as much for what it didn't say about Mourinho as for what it did.

That book contains little background, concentrating entirely on Mourinho's career in football, and, as you would expect from a manuscript endorsed by its subject, nothing that could be construed as criticism.

This book in turn does not concentrate on the negative side of Mourinho's life and career – far from it, as Joel Neto finally managed to point out to Mourinho when he at last got a word in edgeways during that phone conversation. After all, the man has far more supporters than detractors.

"He had heard about the book from another journalist who has been sent a review copy, and he had been given an unbalanced view about what it contained," said Neto. "Mourinho is used to controlling everything to do with his own image. When he called, he thought I would be afraid of him and that he could scare me into submission.

"You have to remember that, in Portugal at that time, Mourinho was treated almost like a god. No journalist would question anything he said, or go against his wishes. He ranted and raved at me and said that if the book was published he would sue me. 'I'll see you in court' were his words.

"He accused me of trying to profit from him. I told him I was a journalist and that I had earned my living for 10 years by writing about other people.

"When he finally calmed down I was able to put my point across – read the book yourself and form your own opinion.

"I told him some of the positive things I had written about him. After that he became more reasonable and said something like, 'OK, we'll see. I'll check it out.' He hung up."

When the book was published Neto sent Mourinho a copy but did not hear directly from him again. However, two months after that, Mourinho's lawyers applied for an injunction to have the book withdrawn from sale.

"There were four particular passages in the book that he contested, and in each case he alleged that I had given him a bad image," said Neto.

"Of course this was untrue. I did not set out to portray him in any specific way, good or bad. I was honest and truthful in writing what others said about him and left my readers to make up their own minds what kind of image he had."

When the case same to court, the judge agreed. In his ruling he said that Mourinho had no reason to contest "this honest journalistic piece of work" and dismissed the application.

The book had already enjoyed several good reviews in Portuguese newspapers, and, boosted by the publicity from the court case, sales soared.

As a reprint quickly followed, Mourinho's family allegedly tried other means to halt its spread. A report in the journal *24 Horas* claimed his mother, Maria Júlia, had attempted to buy up all the copies in the main bookstore in Sétubal and was warning shops not to stock it.

Meanwhile, Mourinho's lawyers tried again to have the book banned by appealing against the court ruling. This appeal was heard by three higher court judges, and once again the verdict was clear – the case was thrown out, unanimously dismissed. And Mourinho was told by the judges that if he wanted to enjoy the advantages of being a public figure then he must get used to the disadvantages, too.

"It was humiliating for him, really," said Neto, who was subsequently threatened with an action for defamation by Mourinho – after all, no one has ever accused him of being a good loser.

Neto says he has heard nothing further. "I've

moved on. Thankfully, I'm not as obsessed with José Mourinho as he appears to be with me."

So here is the English language edition of an intelligent, perceptive book about a fascinating individual, which, if he had had his way, you would have been denied the chance to read. Welcome to the world of José Mourinho – The True Story.

John Sellers
Publisher
August 2005

PREFACE

The thing about José Mourinho that always made him stand out was his family background, the strong opinions that other people had about him and, above all, the way he used psychology.

He spoke to his players and to the press in a totally new way, his ideas and the way he expressed them holding his audience in thrall. He shook people awake and lifted the shutters on Portuguese football, a closed world that was traditionally stuffed with big shots, yes-men, and other, sometimes rather suspect, characters.

Some of those who fell out with him said he was petulant, while others were immediately able to identify in the coach from the port of Sétubal, just south of Lisbon, someone who was exceptional, if idiosyncratic.

Perhaps the most perceptive observers saw him as a human being who got through life by masking an almost pathological shyness with an air of arrogance; a man who tried to get the very best from what was available, and a man who always strove to achieve the maximum possible when it came to results.

This is the story of the man who coached FC Porto to win the UEFA Cup and the Champions League, justifying the name that less well-intentioned people sometimes give him: "The Changer". And it is also the story of the rite of passage of an aristocratic young Portuguese who earned from Russian billionaire Roman Abramovich, owner of Chelsea and friend of Vladimir Putin, the epithet of the next big thing in world football.

INTRODUCTION

On 24 April 2003, at what was then just about the high point of his career, José Mourinho was penalised for obstructing one of the opposition players. Porto were leading Lazio 4-1 in the first leg of the UEFA Cup semi-final in Portugal when the Argentinian Castroman attempted to take a quick throw-in for the visitors.

Mourinho was sitting on the bench when he spotted the danger and instinctively stopped Castroman. He was sent off by the referee and subsequently barred. Thus when the two sides met again 15 days later in the Olympic Stadium in Rome, Mourinho was banned from the dug-out and forced to sit in the stand with a UEFA inspector nearby, checking his movements to prevent him having any contact with his (or anyone else's) players.

The 0-0 draw in the second leg, which sealed Porto's qualification for the final of the UEFA Cup, was orchestrated by Mourinho via a series of messages sent to the bench in the course of the match. He used no fewer than four sophisticated electronic messaging devices, two of them in the hands of assistants André Villas Boas and Lima Pereira, who both sat beside him in the stand, and the other two in the hands of Aloísio and Baltemar Brito, who were in the dug-out.

José Mourinho was able to give vent to his feelings as the game unfolded, as if he were simply another fan, but his words were passed on as text messages to the assistants who were directing operations from the edge of the pitch. And that meant he had to control his emotions and keep a cool, clear head. In the 13 messages sent throughout the 90 minutes of the game, he was always one step ahead of its demands, preparing what he really wanted to say to players and the exact moment he needed to say it.

Before the kick-off, Aloísio received a text message with the first order: "Tell the players where I am, and that I want them to look at me before the game". A few minutes later, Deco, the great midfield strategist, was the focus of his coach's attention: "Keep possession. Deco should play more. Shout" (seventh message); "Deco should stop inventing moves" (tenth message); "Tell Deco that I am watching him. He has to produce a lot more!" (eleventh message).

Still some way from the end, the team was made to feel that the semi-final had almost been won and that one last push was all that was needed. Mourinho ordered: "Start saying that there are only five minutes to go" (14); "Tell them the time again. Total concentration" (15). A little later, his focus was on the linesman, responsible for signalling off-sides when Lazio were attacking: "Put pressure on the linesman, everybody" (16).

When a direct free-kick was awarded against Porto, the instruction to the men forming a defensive wall was typical of Mourinho's almost obsessive attention to detail: "Derlei in the wall instead of Hélder Postiga" (18).

The level of activity near the dug-out grew as more and more players moved next to the touchline, waiting to receive instructions from their coach. "Change the players who are warming up. Tell the guys not to get too excited. Total concentration" (20). "Change substitutes" (21). "Change the people who are warming up" (24). The complete list of messages was reproduced in the first version of *José Mourinho*, the book about the trainer's career from his leaving Barcelona through to winning the UEFA Cup in Seville on 21 May 2003. Luís Lourenço, the author, had access to this list, realised its significance and, without much consideration, published it in full.

That is how things are with José Mourinho: total attention to detail and management of human resources before anything else, in the certainty that people are, and always will be, the most important element in any organisation destined for success. Even on an ordinary day, throughout the two-and-a-half years he was working at Porto, the players were really put through their paces. They would arrive at the Gaia training centre after breakfast, train, have lunch, train some more and only then go home. A simple talk during a training session was delivered with the players lying on their backs on the ground, to avoid distractions. They all received a letter signed by Mourinho, with a note of welcome, a demand for total commitment and the definitive formula for success: "Motivation + Ambition + Team spirit = Success".

Microsoft Portugal chose to include Mourinho in a conference on leadership in 2004. People who attended Mourinho's talk were put in mind of Jesus Christ riding into Jerusalem over palm fronds, with the cheers of the multitude ringing in his ears. "He is a born leader," Rudolfo Oliveira, Communications Director of the Portuguese branch of the company, said.

Deco, the midfield maestro, was never quite as influential at Porto under Mourinho as he had been in the days of the previous coach. Nevertheless, he still maintains that Mourinho is quite simply "the best in the world".

"José Mourinho assembles a core of players who will behave exactly as he wants them to behave and builds a team around them. They create the mould for others," says Rui Santos, former editor-in-chief of the magazine *A Bola* and now a sports commentator.

To do this at Porto, he signed players from "his" Uniao de Leiria team (which he managed before his move to Porto) – Derlei, Nuno Valente, Maciel and the veteran Tiago, whose main function was to ensure that the spirit in the dressing room was right.

"Basically, it was a way to get them all dancing to the same tune, and making them all equally humble. Mourinho is good tactically, and a great student of football, but above all he likes to know exactly what he can expect from his players so that he avoids surprises," adds Rui Santos.

Mourinho does have his superstitions. Before every game he kisses a laminated photograph of his children and a crucifix bought in Bom Jesus de Braga at the end of 2000, during the weekend of a match between Vitória de Guimaraes and Benfica. He kissed them before the Champions League final; he kissed them before an FC Porto-

Moreirense showdown; and he certainly kisses them before a Chelsea-Manchester United clash. It is in this little gesture of kissing a photo of two children and a Roman Catholic symbol that we catch a glimpse for a moment of the man behind the myth.

Mourinho's aunt Mária José Ulke, 59, one of the people closest to him (she helped look after him during the first five years of his life), can see today "the same look" that the young boy wore when he used to cling to her during thunderstorms or when earth tremors shook their home. "He had a sad air about him, didn't he?" says Maria José. "They called the family privileged, but not him. He is the product of a very difficult childhood, full of problems. Of the whole family, he is the best," she says, flicking through a photo album of weddings, family picnics and political gatherings at which members of the family took part. And, slowly, the lines come together that make up the complex map of the route to the head and the heart of José Mourinho, the most surprising and striking personality to emerge on the football scene for many years.

CHAPTER ONE
A FOOTBALLING ARISTOCRAT

"He had a sad air about him, didn't he? They called the family privileged, but not him. He is the product of a very difficult childhood, full of problems. Of the whole family, he is the best..."

MARIA JOSÉ ULKE, aunt

José Mário dos Santos Mourinho Félix was born on 26 January 1963, his baptismal name bearing two of the three genetic markers that would have such an influence on his personality. The "José" comes from his father, José Manuel Mourinho Félix, former goalkeeper for Vitória de Sétubal and Belenses, and one-time Portuguese international, generally known as Félix Mourinho. "Mário" is the first name of Mário Ledo, former chairman of Vitória, a successful businessman who took under his wing his niece and nephew, Maria Júlia and Mário Carrajola dos Santos, the mother and uncle respectively of José Mourinho.

On his father's side, Mourinho's origins were modest. Félix Mourinho's father was the cook on a cruise ship. When he died he left a modest house and a plot of land.

But Mário Ledo was the owner of the Unitas canning factory, Chairman of the Syndicate of the Canning Industry, a partner in a cinema business, and a founder and respected shareholder of Vitória. It was he who gave the club the land where the Sétubal stadium was built. The fact that he did not have any children of his own, combined with a philanthropic nature, which, to this day, has left its imprint on the city, led him to bring into his home, in the Sétubal suburb of Aires, Maria and Mário, two of the four children of Luísa, his sister-in-law, who was then aged 22.

Ledo wanted successors and, because it was impossible to produce an heir of his own blood, he decided to bring up Maria and Mário – two other brothers, both with mental and physical disabilities, were initially excluded–and made them the heirs to his considerable fortune.

Two years after Mário Ledo died, Portugal was in the grip of the 1974 revolution. The right-wing authoritarian regime under which Ledo had prospered was overthrown in a Communist-dominated military coup, which substantially reduced this inheritance. The Unitas factory was occupied by workers and sold at public auction, and practically all that was left for the two heirs was the private property. But there was a fair amount of that; the inheritance tax alone amounted to almost £10,000, a hefty sum at the time – and it was in these comfortable financial surroundings that José Mourinho grew up.

His mother Maria, known as Nené, is now in her late sixties and was originally a primary school teacher. She describes Ledo as "more than a father to me and more than a grandfather to my children."

"Mário [José Mourinho] had a fairly comfortable life, in very nice family surroundings. By the age of 18 he already had his own car."

Maria José Ulke, the aunt married to Mário, from whom she was divorced two-and-a-half years later, was involved in a series of court cases and, not entirely free of public scandal, was the fly in the ointment of the happy family idyll. Her version of the family history is a mass of memories characterised by thwarted ambitions, betrayals and a certain submissiveness on the part of the future coach of FC Porto towards the dominant figure of his mother. Mário Ledo's family was one of the most conservative in the city, and there was resentment towards them from the "new aristocrats" of post-revolutionary Portugal. There was a certain amount of settling of personal scores among folk who felt it necessary to seek out those responsible for an empire that had now collapsed.

Maria José, who after her divorce from Mário gained possession through the courts of the family home in Aires, keeps the furniture and decorations in Mário Ledo's sunny study just as the industrialist left them at the time of his death in March 1972. Pictures of the patriarch fill the walls of the three-storey house – 15 wooden-floored rooms in which Maria José lives with her memories.

The room where José Mourinho and his sister Teresa, who was three years his elder, slept has also been left untouched. The beds are made, and everything is spotless, frozen in time. This is how it was when Maria Júlia moved out in 1968, with Félix Mourinho and their two children, to the Bairro do Montalvao district, within the city limits of Sétubal.

"Zé Mário [José Mourinho] lived with us for five years," said his aunt Maria José. "His parents slept in a house nearby (the Santa Rita residence –

another luxurious property built by Mário Ledo for the family), but they all ate here, which was where the children lived and all the rest of the family, as well as the two servants."

Maria José, who later remarried, added: "My nephew was a treasure. Once there was a great earthquake (1968, a particularly significant moment in the history of the region), and he was terrified and clung on to me. He was very dear to me. I always enjoyed being with him so much. Ever since he was a small boy he has impressed me a lot. His eyes were always lively and attentive; he observed everything around him and understood it all. I think he is the same today – very attentive."

At the age of five, José Mourinho had an attack of appendicitis. It developed into peritonitis and, his life in danger, he underwent an emergency operation followed by two weeks in hospital.

"He was a very loving child," recalls Maria Costa, a neighbour, now 60 years old. "He was about the same age as my daughter, Zélia, and right from the very first he liked to come to my house to play." It was shortly after this that Mourinho and his parents moved to the city. Over time, suburban Aires went downhill. It became dirty and polluted, with a petrol station, a MacDonalds, and a mass of graffiti. But in those days, in the mid-Sixties, it was an upmarket place to live. After moving to Sétubal, José Mourinho revealed the third genetic trait that went to shape his character, this time something of his own. It came from the merging of the competitiveness of his father and the aristocratic nature of his mother – the appetite for leadership. His mother Maria Júlia recalls how "he used to organise his friends with ease – he was giving the orders. He used to organise football games. He only used to come home to drop off his satchel, and then he would be away, always involved with getting the players around here sorted out..."

Luís Lourenço, a childhood friend and now a journalist (and Mourinho's official biographer), was his next door neighbour in those days. The two were barely four months apart in age, and were firm friends, even though they did not go to school together. Lourenço stayed in the state education system, while José Mourinho went to the Diocesan private school, a select and elitist establishment, with palm trees and walls covered with Disney motifs, located at the end of the main avenue in Sétubal. But out in the street everyone was equal, and the two of them spent their teenage years bonded like brothers, a relationship that later prompted Mourinho to invite Lourenço to be best man at his wedding in 1988.

The journalist remembers Mourinho as a sober,

quiet and determined young man. "When he was 15 you couldn't have said that he would become what he is today. As a youngster, his life wasn't any more interesting than mine, or anyone else's. The rest of us got drunk and acted the fool, but he always behaved himself. Now I see that while we were sowing our wild oats, he was observing and learning. To a certain extent, he was a spectator rather than a doer; on the other hand, he was already a leader in embryo."

Mourinho was the moderate one among their circle of friends. He never smoked or drank, he was careful about how he dressed – casual but elegant – and cultured. He never wore earrings or other jewellery, he kept his hair short, and gave the impression of being always alert. Susete Frasquilho, Mourinho's teacher at the Diocesan private school, remembers a quiet boy with a sense of humour and a propensity to play practical jokes on his friends. "He would hide things and then act as if it was nothing to do with him," she remembers.

Mourinho went from private preparatory school to private secondary school and, except for flunking mathematics in the twelfth year, always passed his exams without any difficulty. He was something of a heart-throb and had various girlfriends, up until the time he met his future wife

(Matilde, known as "Tami") at the end of one summer when he was just 17 and she was 14. Their romance blossomed at the Caranguejo discotheque and rapidly became serious. "Tami was Zé's first real love. They were crazy about each other," remembers Vítor Pimpão, a friend from their teenage days.

They married nine years later. Now, a decade and a half on, the marriage is still going strong.

CHAPTER TWO
THE MODEST FOOTBALLER

"We played football for the ISEF [Higher Institute of Physical Education] team. He was technically sound, a skilful footballer, but he wasn't a player with a lot of fight. He didn't like running much."

JOSE PESEIRO, Sporting Lisbon trainer and ex-colleague at ISEF

Football was important right from the start. Mourinho had been swimming since he was four and, by the time he was five, the teachers at the Sétubal's version of the sea cadets were already getting José Mourinho to put on exhibitions of diving as an example for older children. Some days he had to accompany his sister to ballet or riding events, or occasionally go riding himself.

But football was what fascinated him.

"On birthdays and at Christmas he would always ask for various things, but if he didn't get a ball, it was as if he hadn't been given anything," says his mother.

A member of Vitória de Sétubal football club since the day he was born (with membership card number 772), José Mourinho was only four years old when he persuaded one of the family's employees, Amadeu, to build goalposts in the garden of the house in Aires. "There was a basketball court, but what he wanted was a goal. And then he made poor Mr Amadeu, who was very old, go in the goal and try to stop his shots. And they were pretty hard shots, too," says Mourinho's mother.

As a little child Mourinho used to go behind the goal at Vitória where, so the story goes, on training days he would yell encouragement to his father, who was keeping goal.

As he grew up, he retained all his passion for the game. On rainy days he used to play Subbuteo, the table football game, which he greatly preferred to any other indoor activity.

On sunny days he would go out to the Campo dos Arcos, the Field of Goalposts, in Sétubal. At weekends he used to visit his grandmother Luísa (who died when he was still with FC Porto) and go to watch Belenese play after Félix Mourinho had been transferred there.

He used to travel in his father's car in convoy with the fish van, which used to go through the villages with fresh fish. Coming to the conclusion that he did not have what it takes to be a professional footballer could have been traumatic for Mourinho, but his mother says it was not. "He didn't fool himself. That is why, despite his father being a professional player, and later a coach, we always impressed on Mário that going to school was the most important thing of all," says his mother. She always called her son by the name of his aristocratic uncle Mário, while her husband preferred to call him by the nickname of his cousin, Zé . His friends started to call him Zé Mário.

As his mother puts it: "Football was not to be taken seriously, it was an entertainment. Basically, the life of a professional footballer is very difficult. You need to be very focussed if you are going to be really good."

José Mourinho was not "really good" as a player. José Peseiro, the trainer at Sporting, former assistant to Carlos Queiroz at Real Madrid and ex-colleague of José Mourinho at the Higher Institute of Physical Education (ISEF), remembers that, as a footballer, he lacked precisely the element that most characterises his style as a coach today – an almost manic attention to detail.

"We both played for the ISEF team, where we tried out some of the things we had learned in class, and at the same time we were keeping ourselves fit against other university teams. I didn't play much because I was a professional with Oriental, but Mourinho played practically all the time.

"He played in central defence or central midfield. He was technically sound and skilful, but he wasn't a player with a lot of fight. He didn't like running much."

There was an incident at Rio Ave football club, where his father Félix was by now the coach, which underlined Mourinho's limitations as a player and humiliated him into the bargain. As the son of the coach, Mourinho could go to the ground whenever he wished and played regularly for the reserve team on Wednesdays. José Maria Pinho, then president of Rio Ave, takes up the story: "Once, when the team was warming up at Avelade before a game with Sporting Lisbon (which ended 7-1 to Sporting), central defender Figueirado injured himself.

"Félix Mourinho asked if he could play his son instead. I came down from the stand, went to the dressing room, and told the pair of them that José Mourinho was not to play."

He says that both Mourinho and his father got the point, and did not make waves. But even today there are players from that time who describe a real shouting match, with threats of sacking, accusations and counter-accusations. It is probably a myth.

"Félix Mourinho stayed at the club. Today I'm a great friend of the father and the son," states Pinho.

In interviews, José Mourinho usually says that fate played a hand in making him the celebrated manager he is today. Most of the coaches of his generation started to prepare themselves for the job fairly late in life, normally when they came to the end of their careers as players. Mourinho started 10 to 15 years earlier.

"There are a lot of people who start their training at 30-something. I started mine in my twenties, when I had the capacity to learn," he emphasised in one interview, pointing out the problems of changing from footballer to coach. To begin with, former players, especially those who have done well, tend to make a number of mistakes.

As he once put it during a forum discussion on

the Internet: "I am certain that experience as a player is important in other areas. I have spent my life in football; I have been a player; I know how to live in a group, I know how to behave on the pitch, and all that really helps. A player who has a good understanding of tactics and the ability to read the game when it comes to positioning can offer added value later on, as a coach. But none of this is essential in making someone technically brilliant – a great football coach."

That is why, he contends, lack of success as a footballer did not prevent him from holding the record as the youngest championship-winning coach in Portugal. He also points out that neither Louis Van Gaal, who at the end of the Nineties was considered the best coach in the world, nor Carlos Alberto Parreira, who guided Brazil to the World Cup in 1994, were ever great players themselves. The same could be said of Arsenal manager Arsène Wenger.

In fact, even before the row with José Maria Pinho at Rio Ave, José Mourinho seemed to be preparing himself for a career as a coach. At 15, when his father was coaching at Unioa de Leiria, Zé Mário was organising the ball-boys and acting as a gofer for his father, passing on messages to the players during games. When Félix Mourinho was at Uniao da Madeira, his son spied on the Estrela da Amadora team for a week, work that resulted in a detailed report about the opposition, with his mother correcting his spelling and grammar. As father Félix later recalled in an interview: "It was a very important game. We were going to Amadora, and if we could at least get a draw we would be in the running for promotion to the First Division. For a week he watched the training sessions at Estrela, and what he told me, the advice he gave me, meant that we held them to a goalless draw. He told me how the other side played, and how they trained. I was very pleased with his work, and I gave him some money as a reward."

At home, in addition, José Mourinho was helping his father with statistics and various othertasks. He became an expert in providing detailed information about players, not just from Portuguese teams but from clubs in other countries, too.

The dogs at home were given the names of footballers. One of the favourites was called Gullit, after the former captain of Holland, and a predecessor of Mourinho as Chelsea manager.

And, slowly, playing football became more of a hobby than a potential profession. He started to play five-a-side football against other amateurs in Sétubal, and at this level he stood out. Nevertheless, it was a poor idea for a would-be professional, bearing in mind the risk of injury involved in playing on hard pitches against poor players. This lack of care eventually cost him dear.

Mourinho's mother tells the story: "He broke his left arm during a game. He was at secondary school at the time, and continued to play football with one arm strapped to his chest. Then he had another fall and, and to protect the injured arm, he fell on the other one and broke that as well. He was going around with both arms in plaster for an awfully long time."

José Mourinho eventually played in the first team at Sesimbra and at Belenses (in the Second Division), but he was playing to keep fit rather than for any other reason. "I am an intelligent person. I knew that I wouldn't get any higher as a player. The second division was my level," José Mourinho admitted later in a newspaper interview.

From the point of view of someone aiming to be a coach, football was turning into something considerably more serious than just kicking a ball, and this led Mourinho to try for a place at the Higher Institute of Physical Education. This choice bears witness to the determination and perseverance of the man in making decisions about his own life.

Mourinho failed a maths exam, which he had to resit in the following September. By the time he finally passed it, there were no vacancies left on the physical education course that he wanted to join.

This resulted in his mother, who never stopped encouraging his ambitions and urging him to take control of his own destiny, enrolling him on a management course at the Higher Institute of Labour and Commercial Sciences in Lisbon.

But business school was not for Mourinho. He lasted just one day on the course before returning to Sétubal. "He was very apologetic, but he simply didn't like the course. And I had to accept his decision," says his mother.

The following year José Mourinho joined ISEF as a physical education student. He stood out from the crowd both because of his sharpness of mind and the magnetism of his personality

"He was an irreverent student and passionate about football. He was always agreeable and made friends very easily, but at the same time he was very focused," recalls José Peseiro. For four years, Mourinho commuted daily between Sétubal and Lisbon, at the wheel of his grey-coloured Renault 5.

"José Mourinho was an affable and well-educated young man," Nelo Vingada, one of his teachers at the institute, recalls. "He passed the physical education course with flying colours, with football as his specialist subject."

In a short foreword to the book by Luís Lourenço, another of his teachers, Manuel Sergio, has this to say about Mourinho: "Without exaggerating, I would say that my old student at the ISEF already knew more about football than the professor who taught the first level courses at the university. And that man was over 60 and a real football enthusiast!

"I am sorry if the journalists who write exclusively about sport,some of them ignorant and uncultured, can't find more in José Mourinho than a good trainer. He is a good coach in the traditional sense, but he is more than that; he is a new coach, for a new kind of football."

After ISEF, Mourinho attended a training course in Scotland, under the auspices of UEFA, to gain an official diploma as a coach. The course co-ordinator was former Scotland manager Andy Roxburgh, who later congratulated Mourinho in Seville on Porto's victory in the UEFA Cup. Roxburgh says today that he was particularly impressed by his student.

And so the time had come for José Mourinho to go to work.

CHAPTER THREE
INSPIRED BY THE TEACHER

"We were a group in our final year, all girls, all aged 17, and he was a young peacock of 24 or 25, straight out of university. But he wasn't a teacher you could get close to. Some of us used to provoke him, and he seemed to pretend that we didn't exist."

MARIA JOAO CARVALHO, former physical education student

School was Mourinho's next destination. As a form of insurance, he wanted experience as a teacher, and in 1988 he accepted an invitation from the Portuguese Association of the Parents and Friends of the Disabled of Sétubal to work in a special school teaching the mentally handicapped.

Many of the disabled pupils he taught have fond memories of him. On occasions they would go to the training sessions of the Vitória juniors to receive encouragement from the players. "They often asked Mourinho to give a lesson in football," remembers Célia Santos, one of the directors of the association at the time.

"Sometimes the kids would be brought up here so they could spend some time with us. It was a way of integrating them into society," says Nuno Santos, later goalkeeper for Benfica and at that time one of the players for Vitória de Sétubal juniors.

The teacher's abilities improved, and, a year on, Mourinho accepted an invitation to continue. "His work has been characterised by a high level of competence with regard to specific intervention in the area of psychomotor activity and the overall development of the persons with whom he works, consisting of a group of severely mentally deficient children", as the assessment report puts it. "[As a teacher] he had an extremely affectionate relationship with these children, which we consider very important. We therefore consider that it is of value to continue with his engagement," the management committee added.

At the same time, Mourinho was teaching in an ordinary school. Maria João Carvalho, one of his physical education students during 1988-89 at the

Bela Vista Secondary School, also in Sétubal, remembers him as a fair but hard man, who imposed the same demands and the same challenges on all his students.

"We were a group in our final year, all girls, all aged 17, and he was a young peacock of 24 or 25, straight out of university. We all went to gym classes, even those of us who couldn't do gym because we were injured. We simply wanted to get the certificates," says Maria João, now 35, married with a child and working as an administration officer with a graphics company.

"But he wasn't a teacher you could get close to. He was an unsmiling figure, and kept his distance. Some of us provoked him, and he seemed to pretend that we didn't exist," she remembers. "Once he noticed that my friend Paula was wearing earrings and bracelets. He told her to take them off because she wasn't a member of 'some kind of tribe'. He wasn't a person you could have a laugh with, like some of the teachers whom we got to know during our final year. And he used to demand a lot of us, too. He would divide the group in two and make everyone take part. He always gave preference to competitiveness. He would set us a challenge, and he was very brusque if we failed. And we were from the humanities side of the school, my God."

41

Among the boys, he seems to have been more popular. "He actually got on very well with the male students. For us, Mourinho was the leader, and we were always behind him," said Marco Rafael when remembering his time as a pupil of Mourinho.

A little later, in 1988, he took the opportunity to train the youth team of Vitória de Sétubal. The invitation came from Conhé, an old Benfica player. "He seemed to me to be a well-organised young man, a disciplinarian, with a great feeling for football," says Conhé. "Even though he was only 25 or 26, he knew his way around tactics and strategy. He was the son of a footballer and had the aura of confidence that went with that. On the first day he came to meet the players, he showed that he was a person of culture and intelligence, but I had assumed that he would be," says Conhé, who was then (as now) co-ordinator of youth football at the Sétubal club. For three years, José Mourinho trained the youngsters and assisted Jacinto João ("J.J.") who was the main coach of the juniors. The results were not brilliant. Vitória Juniors won the district championship, but were then crushed by the two giants of the south (Sporting and Benfica).

One of those youth players was Carlos Freitas, now an amateur with Sesimbra in the Portuguese

Third Division and owner of a café in Sétubal. He said: "I had come from the Azores very young, barely 17, and it was the first time I had been away from home. Mourinho gave me a lot of encouragement, set me challenges all the time, but it wasn't easy. Even so, I was one of the three who got into the top flight, along with goalkeeper Paulo Sérgio (the only player still playing First Division football) and Beto[now transferred to Palmelense]."

Sitting on the balcony of his café in the Quinta das Amoreiras, just 200 yards from José Mourinho's home, Carlos Freitas, nearing the end of his career, has memories of a life spent hoping for something that never quite happened. All average footballers reckon that they could have had a better career, but in his case it really could have come true. Carlos Freitas was a fresh-faced young man full of promise. But after being loaned out to a succession of minor clubs, his career steadily declined. He went through 13 clubs in 18 years, all the while watching the progress of his old coach in the newspapers and on television. Today, in his roomy, brightly-lit café (called Sabores Meus, or My Flavours), he is occasionally visited by José Mourinho. "He comes in, says hello, has a cup of coffee, and goes again.

"He doesn't have time for anything else. He

only comes here at holiday time. We don't talk about football. He asks me about the family, but never about the club where I'm playing. Nowadays we're friends, not colleagues," says Freitas, with his new son on his lap.

On the day José Mourinho left Vitória, in 1990, Carlos Freitas and his colleagues organised a farewell party. Some of them, he says, cried a lot.

Mourinho, by then aged 27, had been recruited as a specialist in physical training by Estrela da Amadora, and he soon proved his worth. The team included Rebelo, Miranda, Melo, Vital, Duilio, Rui Neves, Baroti. These players were above average, but the team would struggle to stave off relegation, while at the same time competing in the UEFA Cup, for which they had qualified in the previous season after beating Farense in the Portuguese Cup final under the leadership of João Alves.

The start of the season had been promising. Estrela eliminated Neuchâtel Xamax (Switzerland) from the UEFA Cup and almost immediately repeated the process with Charleroi of Belgium. But after that things had begun to go downhill. The Amadora team were relegated to the Second Division, and José Mourinho departed along with coach Manuel Fernandes.

"We had to do something, but it was a very

controversial thing to let them go, because people liked them. They were both very popular," remembers Marques Pedrosa, who at the time was deputy to the president. "In any event, he and Manuel Fernandes made a great team. Manuel was the leader, but Mourinho was learning fast, interested and interesting. He had a good attitude and excellent intellectual training, and he also had the ability to present things in a straightforward way, getting right to the basics. He was going to have a great future."

CHAPTER FOUR
A CROSS
TO BEAR

"Pinto da Costa once told me, in a jokey kind of way, the story about how Mourinho arrived at FC Porto. He told me that he had reached agreement with Robson to take over as coach, and Robson then said to him: 'I've got a problem. There's a lad who was my interpreter at Sporting and who still sticks with me even though I've left. I owe him a debt of gratitude...' Pinto da Costa replied:'Oh, Mister Robson, it wouldn't take more than four hundred Contos [about £1,000] to solve that problem...'"

OCTAVIO MACHADO, ex-coach at FC Porto

Mourinho's future beckoned a year later, after another stint with the youth team at Vitória de Sétubal, and once again it beckoned through

Manuel Fernandes. After becoming Bobby Robson's assistant at Sporting in 1992, Ferrandes persuaded Sporting to employ his old colleague José Mourinho as an interpreter to bridge the gap between the British technical wizard and a line-up that contained a range of different nationalities, including Luís Figo, Emílio Peixe, Stan Valckx, Balakov and Juskowiak.

Today, when asked about Mourinho, Robson says that he "will be friends for ever" with the Chelsea coach, and these days he avoids using the much-maligned expression "interpreter". He says that Mourinho was a "very good and intelligent student of football", and remembers him as an "ambitious, enthusiastic and interested" professional. Nevertheless, interpret was what Mourinho did, passing on Robson's instructions to the players and (more importantly) keeping the manager informed about what the players were thinking and feeling.

And, in truth, Robson has always found it difficult to look upon Mourinho in those days as anything but an interpreter. Even after working for Robson as second assistant at FC Porto and as first assistant at Barcelona, and even after being offered the job of assistant manager at Newcastle when Robson returned to Britain, in spite of everything the two men had gone through together, Bobby Robson remembered Mourinho above all as an interpreter.

"Eight years as an interpreter, and just a little later he had it all as the trainer at FC Porto. Fantastic, meteoric! It's like a fairytale!" said an excited Robson in 2003, in an interview quoted in the magazine *Doze*.

It is true that it was only when he won the first national championship with FC Porto at the endof 2003 that José Mourinho was able to throw off some of the stigma attached to him being described as as an "interpreter".

Even today, some people still bring it up. As Octávio Machado, Porto's former coach, tells it: "Pinto da Costa once told me, in a jokey kind of way, the story about how Mourinho arrived at FC Porto. He told me that he had reached agreement with Robson to take over as coach, and Robson then said to him: 'I've got a problem. There's a lad who was my interpreter at Sporting and who still sticks with me even though I've left. I owe him a debt of gratitude...' Pinto da Costa replied: 'Oh, Mister Robson, it wouldn't take more than four hundred Contos [about £1,000], and less than five hundred, to solve that problem...'

"Pinto da Costa tells the story as a joke against himself – it wasn't me who asked him. And 'lad' is his expression, not mine," Octávio insists.

In Spain, when they went to Barcelona, Robson and Mourinho were often referred to by journalists in a rather scathing way as "Don Quixote and Sancho Panza", or, if the intention was to be more spiteful, as "Simple and Smart".

Robson and his protégé missed out on silverware and major success at Sporting Lisbon, but when they arrived at Porto it was a different story. In three years, Robson and Mourinho won two championships and two Supercups, and started the club on a roll that would eventually lead to five championships in succession, a new record in Portuguese football.

But there was a problem on the horizon in the form Augusto Inácio, who was officially Robson's Number Two. He became involved in a power struggle with Mourinho during a trip to Japan.

Robson, needing an operation on a cancerous growth, missed the trip and Inácio held an important meeting with the players behind Mourinho's back.

When Mourinho found out and confronted his colleague they began trading insults, and some newspapers even claim that they came to blows, although this has never been officially confirmed. "The problem was that one was the assistant coach and the other was the principal coach's favourite," remembers Paulo Barbosa, a football agent who at the time was working closely with FC Porto.

"Inácio had everything on his side to win this war, but he misjudged the situation and in the end he was the one who was forced to leave."

No one gets the better of José Mourinho easily.

Bobby Robson remained blissfully unaware that Mourinho harboured ambitions to become a coach. "He never told me that he wanted to work on that side, although I knew that one day he would get to the top," Robson said later, quoted in the online magazine *Mais Futebol*.

But at the time, Bobby Robson continued to be in the dark about a lot of things regarding his fellow traveller.

"He didn't know that Mourinho had also been a player," recalls José Maria Pinho. "When the two of us were at FC Porto, he invited me to dinner at his home, as a courtesy, and I told him the story about the Alvalade dressing room, when Mourinho was forced to take off his shirt and go back to the bench. Well, Mister Robson was extremely surprised, because he didn't even know that Mourinho had been a player".

During his four years at Barcelona, between 1996 and 2000, José Mourinho went through two clearly distinct phases: the first year with Bobby Robson, when he was the assistant and great confidante of the coach, and the other three years with the Dutchman Louis Van Gaal, who took him on with a certain amount of distrust and who, in the beginning, was not inclined to ask Mourinho for his opinions.

The transition period was difficult, but the man from Portugal did not give up. He brushed off the criticism about excessive 'Dutchification' of the team in Van Gaal's hands, mustering all the patience he could, focusing attention on every detail that his boss overlooked. As time passed, this enabled him to achieve an increasingly important role at the club.

"Robson left to go to PSV, Van Gaal came in, and Mourinho found himself on the staff in a fairly low position," says Louis Rojo, a Spanish journalist who, as the Catalonia correspondent of the sports daily *Marca*, followed events closely over these four years. "As usual, Mourinho knew how to improve his status. First of all, he became the chief observer at the opposition's games, and gave Van Gaal some excellent reports. He became an expert at observing Barcelona's future opponents and noting their strengths and weaknesses."

Nevertheless he found it difficult to develop his relationship with the team. A number of the players were Dutch, and they preferred to communicate directly with Van Gaal, or with other Dutch members of the coaching staff.

In time Mourinho began to assist Van Gaal during matches. The Dutchman knew that it was difficult to get a really good overall view of the game from the dug-out, so he had Mourinho watch from high in the stand, where he had a panoramic view. The two of them were thus able to discuss the game in minute detail via a mobile video link.

"The result was that they won two Spanish championships in three years," continues Rojo, who in the meantime has become a personal friend of Mourinho.

Mourinho did fail in one of the objectives he had set himself – restoring good relations between Louis Van Gaal and Vítor Baía, the former Porto goalkeeper who had fallen out of favour at Barcelona. Baía had suffered injuries and made several high-profile errors, which led to his fall from grace, and had then become locked in a personal conflict with the coach from which neither of them was prepared to back down. Mourinho did his best to heal the breach, but without success.

At the same time as he was building his career, Mourinho was on a voyage of personal discovery. Along with three members of the team – the

Brazilians Ronaldo and Rivaldo, and the Romanian Popescu – he was living in a quiet apartment block in Sitges, a seaside resort about 20 minutes from Barcelona.

It offered Mourinho the same kind of lifestyle he was used to in Sétubal – sea bathing, fresh fish, it even had a seafront similar to Sétubal's. Once he had put his hectic working day behind him, he could dedicate himself to his family, taking long trips along the coast of Catalonia at the wheel of his Volvo estate car. It was during this period that his children Matilde ('Tita', aged eight in 2005) and José Mário ('Zuca', now age dsix) were born.

Mourinho had already overcome one of the greatest challenges he was ever to face in earning the trust and respect of Bobby Robson, who had delegated various tasks to him, such as the planning and execution of training schedules in preparation for matches.

"The first year with Bobby Robson was pretty complicated. He was taking over from Johann Cruijff, who had been in charge of Barcelona for eight years, and the press were highly critical of the Englishman right from the beginning," said Luís Rojo.

"The president, Josep Lluiz Nuñez, had already been thinking about taking on Van Gaal, which meant he saw the Robson/Mourinho combination as merely a short-term solution. But despite everything they won three trophies that first season – the Spanish Cup, the European Supercup, and the Spanish Supercup. They just missed out on the League, which was won by Real Madrid under Fabio Capelo."

Luís Rojo remembers: "Of course, they had the Brazilian Ronaldo in the side, who was only 20 and probably at his peak, which was a big advantage. But Robson and Mourinho showed a great capacity for resilience, the ability to resist pressure, and do things their way. They took the captaincy away from Guardiola, the Spanish international, and gave it instead to Popescu. They withstood the pressure from the press very well, and time proved them right.

"The side was a good one, also including the likes of Bulgarian Hristo Stoichkov and the Dutchman Patrick Kluivert. But it was not an easy team to manage. It needed strength of mind and the ability to communicate well, and a great deal of fast and effective talking, because, with star players of this class, it simply was not possible to apply the principle that the boss is always right."

There were moments when it was hard to be positive. After a Barcelona-Atletico de Bilbao match, following an unexpected altercation in the players' tunnel, the man from Portugal was humiliated when he heard the coach of the Basque team, Luís Fernandez, say at a press conference: "But who exactly is this Mourinho nobody?"

CHAPTER FIVE
THE GHOSTS OF SÉTUBAL

"[I wanted players with] titles: zero; money: little …

After preparing [the 'Bible'] I was finally ready to be a coach."

JOSÉ MOURINHO

Luís Rojo says that, if the clock could be turned back, Barcelona would have chosen José Mourinho as a replacement for Louis Van Gaal in 2000-2001, rather than Serra Ferrer, a man who had climbed the coaching ladder at the club.

Mourinho had been absorbing knowledge all the time like a sponge soaks up water. From Van

Gaal he learned much about training techniques and defensive strategy; from Robson he learned about attacking football, personal contact with the players and, as Mourinho himself says, helping the team pull together in the hour of defeat. Even the superstars at Barcelona, who would often air their own views about tactics during training sessions, had something to offer.

Certainly there are many people in Catalonia who would still welcome the return of the man from Portugal.

During the last year he spent in Spain, however, José Mourinho was a frustrated man. He stayed for the money and because of his obsession with winning the Champions League. Outwardly, he appeared to be content with his role as an assistant coach, but the truth, according to Luís Lourenço, was that the man from Sétubal was privately critical of Van Gaal. and was not afraid of airing his own opinions. Controversially, in an interview given to the *Jornal de Notícias* in the year Barcelona won the Spanish League, he claimed that it was Celta Vigo who deserved to be champions.

At the end of three years with Van Gaal, with one league championship and one Spanish Cup under his belt, Mourinho decided it was time to go home. He was less than impressed by Joan

Gaspart, who had replaced Josep Lluis Nuñez as President.

Van Gaal was about to leave to return to Holland as technical director at Ajax. His successor, Serra Ferrer, made it known that he did not intend to continue with Mourinho, but by then the man from Sétubal had already made it clear that he was planning to leave anyway.

In the dressing room, Van Gaal told the whole team what he thought about Mourinho. "It is the end of the career of a great assistant coach, and the start of the career of a great coach!"

Mourinho was determined that his days as a number two were over. He was invited to rejoin his mentor, Bobby Robson, who had gone back to England to manage Newcastle United, as his assistant– an invitation that generated plenty of publicity and dozens of interviews – but in the end he turned the offer down. There was nothing to indicate that, in the foreseeable future, he would replace Robson as the man in charge. And he was determined to be a number one.

A year before, he had revealed his strategy during one of his regular contributions to the electronic magazine *Mais Futebol*: "It won't be long before I'm back in Portuguese football, and obviously I am going to be paying closer attention to Portuguese teams. Absorbing all the information available will be my number one priority."

In another message, written after the announcement that he was leaving Barcelona, he was even more outspoken: "I'm faced with a situation at work without responsibilities and the burden of living all the time without motivation."

The first thing he did after leaving Barcelona was personal: he went to Orlando in Florida with his daughter, on a long-promised trip to Disney World.

In fact, Mourinho was entering one of the most complicated and difficult periods of his life. His return to Sétubal had brought some traumatic memories to the surface. One of them could be clearly seen on Mourinho's face – a scar on his forehead, caused by a car accident four years earlier when, coming back from Spain for a few days, Mourinho had insisted on driving without a break between Madrid, Oporto and Sétubal, and ended up by coming off the road just outside the town of Sado. More difficult to come to terms with was something Mourinho found himself encountering on every street, in every face and in every word when he came home: the ghost of Teresa, his sister, who had died in 1997 from septicaemia, a complication of the diabetes that had left her practically blind following a short period of drug abuse. Later, when he was coach at FC Porto, he would say that the day Teresa died was the worst day of his life. The pair had slept in the same room for five years, had shared their early childhood games and, as their friends said, they had a very close bond. The photographs of the family – the few known ones, that is – always show them together, often embracing, with the older sister's arm extended protectively around her little brother.

Now unemployed, José Mourinho made it clear that he was open to offers. However, he also made it clear that he would not adopt the approach of some unemployed coaches who, by Christmas, are keenly awaiting –and in some cases lobbying for – other coaches to be sacked.

"I am an acute observer, but I am also a person of ethics and dignity," he told *Mais Futebol*.

He knew that it would not be easy to join a big club immediately, and that was why he lowered his sights a little. His main priority was clear: "I don't want to be just another coach in the heap any longer," he said in an interview with *Jornal de Notícias*.

Job offers did come along. Alverca wanted him to join forces with Mariano Barreto – they were to be jointly in charge – but he turned it down. Then he was tempted by an offer to coach Sporting de Braga, but, while he was considering it, an opportunity appeared to arise at Benfica, historically Portugal's leading club but at this time going through something of a crisis.

Eventually, with the help of football agent Paulo Barbarosa, he signed a contract with Abilio Rodrigues, who was attempting to win control of the club. If Rodrigues was elected president, Mourinho would immediately replace Manuel José as coach. But the man in power, Vale e Azevedo, won the vote and Mourinho's hopes were dashed.

"Nowadays I would seize with both hands some of the offers I had in the past," he admitted in an interview with *Publico*.

"Portuguese football is a place where I can move around practically with my eyes closed, where there are no secrets or pitfalls for me," he said. Mourinho liked to discount the notion that the high point of his career had been as assistant coach at Barcelona, but nevertheless recognised the truth of it when he said: "It takes a lot more skill and quality to be number two on Wall Street than number one on the Lisbon stock exchange."

Today, José Mourinho says the time he spent

waiting for the right job to come along was the most profitable of his career. At home in Sétubal or on holiday in Ferragudo, he invested the time in his own training, devouring books, videos, DVDs and Internet sites about football. And it was at this time, too, that he put together his "Bible", a lengthy book in which he describes, with the aid of computerised presentations, everything he knows about coaching, and where and how he learned it.

Later, a part of this file would be sent to Pinto da Costa, at the end of Mourinho's first season as coach at Porto. But Mourinho has insisted that no part of his bible should ever be published. So the world will probably never see this day-to-day record of every training session he participated in since he started work with Manuel Fernandes in 1990.

It is a reminder of the vast amount he learned at Sporting Lisbon with Roger Spry and Terzinski (English and Bulgarian physios respectively) and, at the same time, he contends that in the modern technical structure there is no place for the traditional physio.

Here are all the objectives to be achieved, with the training methods and tactics needed to attain every one of them.

Here are Mourinho's ideas about how to bring on younger players in Portugal, signing them from minor clubs and keeping them on low wages – keeping them hungry.

"[I wanted players with] titles, zero; money, little," as Mourinho remarked in an interview with *Jornal de Notícias* in January 2004, lifting the veil a little on his approach to building a team.

CHAPTER SIX
THE DAYS
OF CHANGE

"He wasn't an easy person to get on with, either; he was opinionated, said anything that came into his head, and at the beginning his arrogance was a shock to the whole team. But after a while we got to like him. If he thought the team was weak, that was his right. But not everything was negative."

PAULO MADEIRA, footballer

When the phone call came one September evening from his friend Eládio Paramés, previously a journalist with *A Bola* and at that time working with Benfica, Mourinho finally knew that what he had been striving for was fast approaching.

Jupp Heynckes was on his way out as Benfica's coach, and Paramés told José Mourinho that he wanted to meet him as soon as possible, at his office in the Avenida da Liberdade in Lisbon. The aim was to offer him a six-month contract with automatic renewal for two years at the end of that period, and to introduce him to the President, who would be up for re-appointment in the elections scheduled for that autumn.

Mourinho, the youngest Portuguese coach ever to work at Benfica, and the second youngest of all after the Swede Sven-Göran Eriksson, now England manager, arrived without the support of the fans.

He started as coach with a defeat by Boavista and then became involved in arguments with a number of the players, dropping some who were idols of the supporters, such as Sabry, Calado, Kandaurov, and Chano. He antagonised a number of young players by saying they had no future – Miguel, Carlitos, Diogo Luís, Geraldo and Nuno Abreu, whom their older colleagues started to call the "shrapnel brothers" because of the hardness of the training and their low wages.

He got upset about the signing of players he had not endorsed, such as Rui Baião, Ricardo Esteves, Roger and André. And he stuck to his guns when other officials at the club questioned his training methods.

He had other difficult situations to handle, such as rumours about a homosexual relationship between a singer and the midfielder Calado (who even walked out of a game at half-time, upset by the claims).

To begin with, Mourinho's results were modest, but he surprised everyone by crushing rivals Sporting Lisbon 3-0 in a memorable derby match in December 2000, and, when he did come to leave, the Benfica fans were sad to see him go.

Carlos Mozer, former Brazilian international and Benfica icon of the Eighties and Nineties, was Mourinho's assistant during his short stay with the club, and he remains a big fan. He said: "It had been a long time since I had seen a coach who was as organised as he was, and knew as much about the kind of training needed to improve this or that particular point, whether it was at the technical, physical or psychological level. It was a great day for football when José Mourinho became a head coach. I hope one day I will work with him again."

In the book *José Mourinho*, however, Mourinho stresses what went wrong at Benfica rather than what went right. They were against him from the beginning, he would claim later, but still without identifying exactly who 'they' were. In interviews and conversations since that time, Mourinho has often expressed his frustration with what he saw as the lack of organisation at Benfica, accusing the management, and in particular António Simões, the Director of Football, of betraying the team by failing to sign players of the necessary quality. Mourinho also complained about mistakes made in other areas of the club associated with his own sphere.

For example, he criticised the man whose job it was to spy on the opposition and report back ahead of the game. Peres Bandeira had been studying the Boavista team and gave a detailed presentation at which, however, he only talked about 10 of the players. The one he didn't mention, Erwin Sanchez, turned out to be the key man in Benfica's defeat. This compelled Mourinho, acting on his own initiative, to bring in an old contact from college days to do the job instead.

Referring to the team, Mourinho has since said that it was made up of "old men and foreigners of dubious quality," that they "didn't work much," and that they were "used to losing." Despite the fact that a considerable number of the team were full internationals, he claimed they were "an ordinary bunch of players," the only exceptions being Meira, Marchena, Enke, and Van Hooijdonk. Of some of the others, he claimed their attitude towards their daily work was so laid back that they would even turn up for training without shin-pads.

Paulo Madeira, one of the central defenders and later the captain, regrets the way the book portrays the team. "José Mourinho has only bad things to say about us in the book, but it wasn't all bad. He doesn't mention, for example, that when the news broke that he was going, we all got together and went to the office of the President, Manuel Vilarinho, to try to persuade him to keep him on as coach," he said.

Mourinho, however, denied this in an interview in *Record* in December 2000, maintaining that he declined the support of the players and made the offer to leave to the President.

The players selected by Mourinho in the first team he picked were: Robert Enke, Dudic, Paulo Madeira, Ronaldo, Rojas, Fernando Meira, Maniche, Carlitos, Poborsky, Sabry, and Van Hooijdonk. Curiously, none of these players was still at Benfica two years later.

Madeira claims there was plenty of talent available. He said: "I do find it strange that he regards everything as so negative. It wasn't. He wasn't an easy person to get on with, either. He was opinionated, said anything that came into his head, and, at the beginning, his arrogance was a shock to the whole team. But after a while we got to like him. He had some good methods of working – he was up-front, and he was ready to admit that he sometimes got things wrong.

"Once he made a gesture which touched us a lot. He discovered, while watching a training session at one of the club schools, that the father of one of the lads had died. He asked the boy to come and spend a week with us, to cheer him up."

"If he wanted to think the team was weak, that was his right. But not everything was as bad as he made out. And some of the players from that team were sad when they read what he said about them in that book."

The friction between Mourinho and Sabry was intense. As far as Mourinho was concerned, the Egyptian personified all that he felt was wrong with African football. He was talented, but had shown himself to be precocious and egotistical, in Mourinho's view, and he dropped him.

When the Egyptian complained to journalists, the manager told them how often Sabry lost the ball, how rarely he recovered possession and referred to the eight minutes and three boot changes Sabry had needed before coming on as a substitute. Shortly afterwards the player moved to Maratimo.

But the newspapers had other things to gossip about as well. One story had Marchena, the Spanish central defender, finding himself forced to deny a statement in an interview given to a Spanish newspaper that indicated that Mourinho did not like him. Another incident involved Maniche. One day, after throwing him out of a training session, Mourinho is supposed to have eyeballed him and said: "Yesterday, you managed 800 metres in eight minutes. That means one of two things: either you've got a problem with your head, which you need to get sorted out, or you've got a physical problem, which you need to sort out, too. And because of that, you're going to train with the reserves."

The most curious thing about this is that the player, who some days later apologised, went on to be captain of the team and later became a key figure for Mourinho at FC Porto.

Maniche does not remember this incident. "We did clash once or twice, but it was because we were similar personalities, and we both really wanted to win. My low point at Benfica was before José Mourinho came along," Maniche recalls.

"Mourinho was always understanding, competent and a hard worker at every level. He was demanding, tough and had his principles. He did everything his own way but took a great deal of trouble over me, which did me a lot of good. I owe him everything in my career."

Mourinho was in a difficult situation. He had good relationships with most of the other members of the coaching staff, but, in the short term, Benfica's ambitions were modest. The plan was to identify young players of potential and build a team for the future.

In November, however, Mourinho found himself facing the sack. Chairman Manuel Vilarinho, who, during his electoral campaign, had made no secret of the fact that he wanted to replace Mourinho as coach with Toni, announced that his initial six-month contract would not be renewed.

Nevertheless, the fans began to warm to Mourinho as Benfica's results improved, culminating in that 3-0 victory over arch rivals Sporting Lisbon in December. Mourinho felt it gave him the bargaining power to demand a new contract. Playing a game of all or nothing, he called the Director of Communications, João Malheiro, after the match. Mourinho demanded that the club renew his contract immediately, and asked for a brief meeting with Vilarinho.

"The decision must be taken now," he insisted, and mentioned that there had been an offer from 'another club'.

Vilharinho said: "As far as I was concerned, he could have had a contract for another year, but the shareholders wouldn't go along with it." This was the message Mourinho got from the president when he finally agreed to a meeting.

José Mourinho was disappointed and angry. He told the newspapers: "Vilarinho has no power at the club." And he accused the president of using "the shareholders" as a way out.

Later, in the book by Luís Lourenço, Mourinho apologised for this remark, saying that he had assumed there had been a kind of "blackmail" applied to Vilarinho, which needed to be brought out in to the open. "Vilarinho is a good man who didn't deserve the treatment he got. The accusations made against him were unfair and unjust," says Mourinho, and points out that, in any event, it was he himself who finally made the decision to leave.

At that time, incidentally, his record was rather ordinary by Benfica's standards: 12 games, six wins, four draws, and two defeats, including a distressing elimination from the UEFA Cup at the hands of Halmstads of Sweden. Benfica drew 2-2 at home after losing the first leg 2-1 under the previous coach, Jupp Heynckes.

In truth, it had been clear for some time that Mourinho's relationship with Benfica would end sooner rather than later. When the club beat Campomaiorense 3-0 he made a point of dedicating the victory to Vale e Azevedo, the president who had originally signed him before losing out to Vilarinho in the election. "It was a mistake to carry on after the elections," Mourinho was to admit later.

CHAPTER SEVEN
A STEP BACKWARDS

"With all due respect to Uniao de Leiria, I realise that it was a temporary solution. As far as Mourinho was concerned, going to Leiria wasn't the same thing as going to a major club. And it wasn't easy to firm up the deal either, because João Bartolomeu had serious doubts about giving him a contract. He took a lot of convincing."

JOSÉ VEIGA, former football agent.

The "other club" that Mourinho claimed had made an offer to him when he was at Benfica was local rivals Sporting Lisbon. They let coach Augusto Inácio go on the same day that Mourinho met with Vilarinho, something that Mourinho still insists was "just a coincidence."

Sporting's general manager, Luís Duque, wanted Mourinho as coach, but he met huge opposition from within the club. The fans, who had watched Mourinho repeatedly punch the air at every goal Benfica scored against Sporting the previous weekend, were against him, too.

So, as Luís Duque was later to lament: "Sporting lost the chance of having a coach who was entirely committed; an ambitious coach, with a proven track record of success. Mourinho had leadership qualities, was a very hard worker, and, without being rude about the 'old school', started a new era in training techniques in Portugal."

But the result was a new period of unemployment for José Mourinho, exacerbated by the fact that José Veiga, the agent involved in the negotiations with Sporting, had failed to get him any financial compensation when the deal collapsed.

Mourinho went home to Sétubal for a few months, and played one club off against another. In one interview, he announced that he wanted to return to Benfica. On another occasion it was alleged that he had been promised the coach's job at FC Porto. In the meantime, he was said to be dreaming about going back to Spain.

Atletico Madrid, struggling to recapture past glories, were interested in him. But a foreign coach needs a minimum of two years' experience at the top level in his own country before he is allowed to work as a number one coach in La Liga, the Spanish Premiership, and Mourinho clearly did not have sufficient experience to meet this requirement.

Without a job, without an income and without any solid prospects, the man from Sétubal found himself forced to accept a more modest invitation. Uniao de Leiria was a minor club, with little history of success. When the supporters went to watch them play, it was said, they always took a radio with an earpiece so they could listen to how Sporting Lisbon were getting on.

"With all due respect to Uniao, I realise that it was a temporary solution. As far as Mourinho was concerned, going to Leiria wasn't the same thing as going to a major club," says José Veiga, the agent who set up the deal.

"And it wasn't easy to firm up the arrangements either, because João Bartolomeu (the Uniao President) had serious doubts about giving him the job. He took a lot of convincing."

Mourinho was invited to join the club before the end of the 2000-2001 season, and he thought twice about it himself. Under coach Manuel José, Uniao Leiria was in seventh place in the championship table – they would end up fifth – and, with the resources available at such a club, it would be difficult to do any better. There was no money to take on Carlos Mozer as assistant, and Mourinho was about to lose his first great number two.

When told that the President was planning to replace him with Mourinho, Manuel José stormed: "If Mourinho thinks that this is some kind of jungle and he's Tarzan, he's got another think coming." But 'Tarzan' decided to take the job.

On the day he introduced himself to the players at Uniao, Mourinho told them: "I have no doubt at all that sooner or later I will go to a big club. If you help me to achieve this I will take some of you with me."

A little later, on the club website, he wrote, before a game against his old club Benfica: "With four players from Leiria, I could turn Benfica into champions."

A few months after that, he was working at FC Porto, leaving Uniao de Leiria in fourth place, one point off third with just three defeats during his time as coach – against Boavista, Varzim and FC Porto. Four of his Leiria players, Derlei, Paulo Ferreira, Nuno Valente and Tiago, would shortly follow him to Porto.

During his short time at Unaio, Mourinho built a platform for continued success, introducing a much more professional approach, and resisting demands for the team to play an excessively attacking game. He also ended the tradition of always picking the President's son-in-law, centre defender Paulo Duarte, and on the coaching side he encouraged the man he says was his "most brilliant disciple", Vítor Pontes, who became his successor as coach.

Once at FC Porto, he arranged for his personal mobile phone to play a particularly ironic call tone – Tarzan's jungle cry, a wry reference to what he later said was "the most entertaining moment" of his entire career as a professional football coach.

Before he left Unaio, there were two new offers from Benfica. The first came from Vilarinho, who, incidentally, had asked him to withdraw the accusation that he had no power at the club. He met up with Vilharinho, but the Benfica President refused to agree to a list of demands over assistant coaches and the signing of new players, so Mourinho declined the offer.

The second approach came from Vale e Azevedo, who was still intent on regaining the presidency. This deal was again negotiated by José Veiga. Mourinho wavered, but both his mother and his wife persuaded him against it, on the grounds that Veiga had failed to pull off the deal with Sporting. On 28 December 2001, Mourinho sent a laconic message to the agent's mobile, unilaterally putting an end to an official relationship that had lasted 10 years. "I'm staying with Leiria at the moment, but I have other things in mind," was all he would say.

He then got in touch with another agent, Jorge Baidek, who had contacted him earlier, and signed up with FC Porto. At the time, José Veiga called him "a person whose word means nothing", incapable of being "loyal and honest", but later he apologised.

"We now have an excellent relationship, contrary to what some people may think. People have short memories, but I was the first person to stick my neck out for Mourinho, both at Benfica and at Leiria," said Veiga, who has since become sports director at Benfica.

"Any club in the world would be pleased to have José Mourinho. It was he who brought FC Porto out of the shadows. If it hadn't been for him, God knows what would have happened to that club. He is the only coach in the past few years who was really worth anything."

It was at FC Porto, the club Mourinho said he loved to play against when he was assistant at Barcelona, that everything happened for him. In his second year they won almost everything – the Portuguese League and Cup, the UEFA Cup, the

Candido de Oliveira Supercup. The third year was at least as good – the League again, and, despite losing in the final of the Portuguese Cup, a glorious win in the Champions League.

Rui Santos, the commentator, recognises the coach's skills, but emphasises the significance of the timing of his arrival at the club. "It's important to remember that he arrived at FC Porto when the club was at a low ebb, which meant on the one hand that they couldn't really do any worse and, on the other, that they were really anxious to do better. The question of timing is very important in this respect." However, as quoted in the book *José Mourinho*, the Porto President Pinto da Costa maintains that he always saw Mourinho as "a great coach, and, even more, a great leader."

From the day he turned up at the Antas Stadium and heard Mourinho say, "I am certain that we are going to be champions next year," the President was convinced he had found the right coach for the club.

Later, when news broke that Russian billionaire Roman Abramovich wanted to lure his coach away to take over at Chelsea, Pinto da Costa made Mourinho an offer unique in Portuguese football. Even though Mourinho was under contract to Porto until 2006 (he had signed an extension after the UEFA Cup victory) da Costa offered to make him the manager, in the style of English managers, with the authority not only to run the team, but to dictate the way that everything at the club was run.

CHAPTER EIGHT
FC PORTO

"Rubbish/You're rubbish

Play the ball, clowns/Play the ball..."

SUPER DRAGONS – FC Porto supporters

Things were not easy at FC Porto in the beginning. When Mourinho arrived at Antas in January 2002 the team was in decline, out of contention for major honours, and with the stands regularly echoing to chants of "rubbish... you're rubbish" and "play the ball, clowns... play the ball". They had lost three and drawn one of their last four matches; they were in fifth place in the Portuguese League and practically eliminated from the Champions League.

But Mourinho was not put off. He encouraged the players to learn the chants by heart and tried them out one after another in the dressing room; he wanted his players to be stung by the abuse from the fans, and to respond positively.

Mourinho took control of his players' lives. He dictated what they should eat and how they should spend their leisure time, and he started to prepare a series of tactical changes which, in the final analysis, played a big part in putting the club back on top. Above all else, he started to make his mark by exhibiting his extraordinary skills as a master of mind games, a gift that he had exploited in the past, and that would now start to come into its own.

In 2001, a week before a crucial match between FC Porto and Benfica, Manuel Vilarinho announced that he had had a dream in which the Lisbon club would go to Antas and win 3-0. Mourinho photocopied the newspaper article that reported this great "prophecy" and pinned it up in the dressing room, so that the players would see it every day and be stung into action. The tactic – assimilate the negative and turn it into a positive – worked. FC Porto ended up winning 3-2.

When it came to criticising players, Mourinho would sometimes do this in public and sometimes in private, depending on the reaction he anticipated from the player in question and what he felt would achieve the best result.

Agents of individual players were discreetly discouraged from turning up during training sessions, as Mourinho sought to reduce their influence at the club.

The revolution in training methods and the changes in tactics were also important. Along with a total of six assistants (Baltemar Brito, Aloísio, Silvino, André, Rui Faria and Lima Pereira), as well as a series of other people brought in to help, José Mourinho started virtually to live his life at the Gaia Training Centre. He would arrive an hour-and-a-half before training started so he had time to sketch out every work session, monitor the medical condition of the players and, finally, to read the newspapers carefully. Nothing was left to chance: he even checked out how long the grass was.

In matches Porto adopted a new system, switching from 4-3-3 to 4-4-2 most of the time. Mourinho dictated that defenders, midfield players and forwards should play close together, pressurising opponents in their own half of the field.

His team was built around a midfield diamond formation, with the hard-tackling Costinha at the base, the main play-maker Deco ahead of him, with Maniche and either Alenichev or Pedro Mendes on the flanks. As the opposition became used to this strategy, a number of variants were introduced between 2003 and 2004.

When it was time to take centre stage, Mourinho never hesitated. In the match at Benfica that would decide the championship in 2003, he led out his players to a cacophany of abuse from the home fans, who blamed him for the 'treachery" of his departure from Benfica a year before.

It was another well-thought-out tactic. By attracting the volley of abuse, he took some of the pressure off his players, and he experienced a sensation that he has craved ever since: the general, enraged whistling and howling turns him on, makes him feel the focus of attention, makes him feel like "the most important person in the world".

When things were going really well, Pinto da Costa and Mourinho seemed to communicate without speaking, and the President had no reservations about what a brilliant job Mourinho was doing.

"This FC Porto is as good as Vienna," he once said, referring to the Porto side that had lifted the European Cup in Austria in 1987.

José Mourinho got used to talking up his team, too, and it was with a touch of personal pride that he watched more and more clubs try to copy his way of playing. Towards the end of his time with FC Porto, he made the following, heavily ironic, comment: "One coach asked if he could come and watch me at work for a month. Then he tried to do the same thing with his team that I do with mine. But when he was interviewed by the press he said that he had learned nothing from me. Simply watching me at work was enough for him to conclude that he was a modern coach who thought the same way I did." He did not mention any names.

He was also happy to boast: "Almost all the detail that went into the final part of my work for my degree has been turned into a blueprint that is used as a basis for methods of working at FC Porto. And I'm nothing more than a physical education student."

He was offended when his FC Porto team was likened to the hard and efficient Boavista team that won the Portuguese championship in 2001. "Good God, you can't make comparisons like that. That gets me right in the gut. Comparing my FC Porto with Boavista? Right in the gut," he said during an interview.

Mourinho continued to work on the minds of his players, convinced that great performances depended on the right mental approach. He was ever the football psychologist, seeking to get the best out of each individual player. Sometimes he would metaphorically pat players on the head and at other times he would aim a few hefty kicks at the litter bins in the dressing room during the interval. One moment he might be shaking the players up, the next clucking over them like a mother hen. If they failed to live up to expectations, they might be given the cold stare, or be asked to take a seat in Mourinho's office while he explained to them the reasons why he would have to drop them if they kept on doing the things they were doing. Everything was done with the aim of presenting the right psychological challenge to the right person at the right moment for that person.

Even his assistants went through it. Silvino Louro, for example, gained a reputation for being unlucky, which in an atmosphere as superstitious as football is about as bad as a reputation can get. In fact the statistics showed that FC Porto had seldom won when the goalkeeper trainer was allowed to sit on the bench. Mourinho made him join the team for a match against Warsaw, which FC Porto won 6-1, to end the superstition once and for all.

Like Sabry and Maniche before them, other players experienced the sharp edge of the coach's tongue as Mourinho sought to weed out players he reckoned lacked the mental strength or the hunger to be successful. He was scornful of those who were "content with the life they had" and to whom "it didn't matter whether they won or lost, whether they won things or not."

Ricardo Sousa, later a mainstay at Boavista, was summarily dismissed by FC Porto because Mourinho did not believe he had the right psychological make-up. Hélder Postiga, who later became a big-money flop at Tottenham, was once sent off during a game in which FC Porto lost to Belenenses. Mourinho told him: "You won't play for me again!"

Cesar Peixoto found himself in hot water after giving a newspaper interview in which he asked for more time on the field. Vítor Baía, Mourinho's best friend from Barcelona days and the man whom he spent his first year training when he was Robson's assistant at Porto, gave an interview to *Record* in which he also demanded to be allowed to play more, and was confronted by Mourinho in front of the rest of the team. When Baía said: "Remember what I know about you from Spain", he found himself on the end of a disciplinary procedure. Later he apologised to his team-mates and to the trainer, explaining the interview by saying the usual things: it was the journalist's fault, twisting words that had been well meant.

Mourinho continued to be tough with anyone he felt was not toeing the line, regardless of how successful the team was. South African striker Benni McCarthy was dropped after a night out in Vigo, where he had gone to celebrate his girlfriend's birthday two days before an important match against Benfica. McCarthy was forced to apologise to his team-mates, and then backed this up with two goals in a brilliant display against Manchester United in the Champions League. In April 2004, Brazilian Carlos Alberto turned up late for a training session because he had been seeing members of his family off at the airport and they had been held up by immigration officers. Despite numerous pleas for forgiveness, he was left out for the next match and sent to train with the reserves.

However, many of the 'victims' of Mourinho's disciplinary regime ended up admitting that he was right. Carlos Alberto, for example, called José Mourinho "insensitive", but a few days later he said in contrition: "It is in situations like these that people grow."

Today Mourinho is still convinced that when Hélder Postiga eventually looks back on his career he will say of his old coach: "that fellow was a pain, but he liked me and helped me grow. I have to thank him."

Octávio Machado, the coach who was fired by Porto to make way for Mourinho, believes that many of his successor's early problems could have been avoided.

"José Mourinho was a fool, and the only reason he had such a frustrating first year was because he didn't carry on with clearing the dead wood out of the team, a job which I had started. Porto could still have been champions that first season, if he had finished what I had begun. But instead he brought back players I had dropped (Rubens Júnior, Nelson, Pavlin, for example), and he even chose Pavlin to take penalties, simply to try to prove that I had been wrong about everything.

"A few weeks after saying that he had the best team in the world and promising that they were going to be champions, he had to recognise that he only really had five or six players. Honestly, this is the best compliment anyone has paid me in my entire career," says Machado.

"When I went to FC Porto, the club had not been title contenders for two years, and were not even in the Champions League. I was used to winning, but I was left to sort out a whole series of blunders. The team still had the same basic framework it had had seven years before, and the club had a very poor record of signing players in the transfer market. There was a massive imbalance in the team, which I tried to deal with during the time I was there.

"Agents acting for individual players had too much influence, the chairman was weak, and, as a result, the squad was poorly assembled. The clearance I started served José Mourinho well later on, and he ought to acknowledge that."

What José Mourinho did "acknowledge" in 2002 was that FC Porto had an "entirely inadequate management structure" which, he said in an interview with a Spanish newspaper, was responsible for producing "the worst FC Porto team for the last 26 years."

Octávio claims he has "nothing against Mourinho", but neither can he forget the events which led to his replacement as coach of FC Porto. According to his version , on 21 January 2002, shortly after his team had been knocked out of the Portuguese Cup by Sporting Braga, and following a defeat by Boavista in the championship, Pinto da Costa swore that rumours about him negotiating with José Mourinho were untrue.

That same evening he publicly admitted during a TV discussion that Octávio was history, and Mourinho could be the immediate future.

Next evening, Pinto da Costa and several other senior figures at the club met Mourinho at a restaurant. The gathering was broadcast direct by television cameras in the street outside.

Octávio said: "I respect José Mourinho as a coach and tactician. But I do want to say that I don't think he has brought anything new to Portuguese football. This isn't the first time that FC Porto have been European champions.

"Mourinho is extremely ambitious and well prepared. He does some great work, but he can only seize the opportunities that are presented to him, and therefore he is just as limited as many people who have gone before him."

"On ethical grounds I must take him to task. He has no respect for individuals or institutions. He made a personal attack on Manuel José when he went to Leiria, then he made accusations against Manuel Vilarinho at Benfica, and he signed a contract with FC Porto – or at least reached an agreement to sign a contract – while I was still the club coach," he said.

"Mourinho was always aiming for the top in Portuguese football, and for the first time this really gave him the opportunity to go for it. I would have been incapable of behaving like that, but for him that kind of thing was normal.

"He plainly benefited and learned from being with Robson and Van Gaal, but at that time he showed no sign that he was destined for the top."

The rest of the 2001-2002 season was frustrating as far as José Mourinho was concerned, with a mixed bag of results on the pitch and a lack of consistency. But he had started to prepare for the future, bringing in players he had carefully selected (Maniche and Pedro Emanuel, as well as the four who followed him from Unaio – Paulo Ferreira, Derlei, Nuno Valente and Tiago).

He also identified players he would sign in the future (Jankauskas and Cesar Peixoto) and the players he would need to replace (Pena, Ricardo Silva, Paulo Santos). And he stamped his authority on the team, even being prepared to drop his superstar Deco if he deemed it necessary.

He accused the Portuguese football establishment of favouring Benfica, who were Porto's main rivals for a place in the following season's UEFA Cup. In the end, Porto finished third in the championship table, which meant they had clinched that important place in the European competition, which would provide the springboard for the glory days ahead for Mourinho. His view today is that it was a satisfactory start and the results the following season proved that his strategy was correct.

The season ahead would later be described by Pinto da Costa as "the best year" in the history of FC Porto, a club which had, in the past, won the European Cup, the European Supercup and the Intercontinental Cup. If the seeds of the success to come were sown by Mourinho in the spring of 2002, they continued to grow through the summer as the players trained together, got to know each other better, and slowly but surely built team spirit

One of the most valuable techniques that Mourinho taught his players was what he called resting with the ball – the ability to get the ball under control and then 'rest' with it at their feet, keeping possession by passing it between players while they recharged their batteries. The Porto players did get weary as they relentlessly pursued the championship. But although the championship continued to be the main objective, it became apparent that the UEFA cup was becoming more than just a dream.

Mourinho had his own way of dealing with the occasional defeat, and if things went wrong he used to think back to what he had learned from horseriding, from the lessons he shared with his sister more than 30 years before. "Whenever you fall off a horse, the first thing you have to do is get back on, so you overcome the fear immediately. If you put it off until tomorrow, you'll never get back on." Every time Porto lost a game, Mourinho wanted the next game to come quickly so there would never be time for defeatism to set in.

Porto won their first trophy under Mourinho when they wrapped up the Portuguese League championship with two matches remaining. By that time they had already seen off Lazio in the semi-finals of the UEFA Cup (when Mourinho was banished to the stand) and it meant they could prepare for the final without the distraction of domestic competition. Mourinho was able to rest his entire first team from the final two league matches.

And so it was on to the Olympic Stadium in Seville, filled to capacity and with fans going wild, where Mourinho's team beat Celtic 3-2 after extra time to lift the UEFA Cup.

"Finals are intended to be won," Mourinho told the players the day before the big match. As they left the dressing room, he yelled at them: "Who are we?" and they yelled back: "Porto!" And so it went on: "Who are we?" "Porto!" "Who are we?" "Porto!"

Porto took the lead through Derlei, but Swedish striker Henrik Larsson equalised for Celtic. Alenitchev put Porto ahead again, Larsson equalised again, and the match went into extra time. As the minutes ticked away Mourinho prepared himself mentally for a penalty shoot-out – he had even chosen the players who, in his mind's eye, would score the first five for Porto – but the team didn't let him down, and Derlei scored again. This time Celtic could not respond.

In the personal account that he wrote about that fantastic night in Seville, José Mourinho refers to his most important players by the nicknames by which they were known to their team-mates off the pitch. Deco is The Magician, Derlei is The Ninja, Jorge Costa is The Bug, and Costinha is The Minister.

The rest of his version of events is largely a tapestry of personal and family memories,which is unusual for him: how nervous his wife was, how anxious his father was, the confidence his children had. "That day I stopped being just a coach known in Portugal, and became a coach known throughout the world," is how Mourinho himself ends the story.

There was one final chapter to be written before the end of a remarkable season. After a two-week break, Porto went on to clinch the Portuguese Cup against his 'old friends' Uniao de Leiria. Derlei was injured in training and seemed likely to miss the match. But the Ninja made it... and once again scored the decisive goal.

CHAPTER NINE
MANAGING THE IMAGE

"He would visit us at Christmas and, when he came to Oporto, if we had the chance we would have a coffee together. Sometimes it would happen that we were all together, including my partner. He never had anything negative to say about my views. We've never talked about me being gay."

JOÃO MÁRIO, cousin

Another facet of José Mourinho's growing success was his strict management of his own image and careful handling of the press. "I realise that my image could be better, but one of my flaws is not to give a damn about it," he once told an Internet newspaper.

Mourinho admits it: newspaper, radio and

TV interviews are prepared for in detail, responses at the press conferences are worked out beforehand, and public statements often used to get a message across to a third party. For example, Mourinho always handled his relationship with the Portuguese national team coach, Luís Felipe Solari, through the media. In a typical newspaper interview, there would be with an opening compliment to Solari, followed by a barrage of criticism and, at the right moment, Mourinho would demand the release of his players from the national squad so they could play for Porto.

Intelligence, wit and cunning are all used when a notebook or microphone appears. Before a match between Porto and Sporting Lisbon, journalists asked Mourinho to name his team. He declined, but offered instead to name the Sporting team. His forecast of who, and how, the opposition would play was exactly right, and once again the press made much of this.

Many reporters in search of an interview with Mourinho would be forced to run the gauntlet of a series of Porto officials before receiving a reply by fax or email. They were often worded something like this: "Professor José Mourinho is obliged to advise you that he is not available for the interview requested," and signed by one of the press officers, Antero Henriques or Acaio Valentim.

Some of the pithier Mourinho comments came from the pitch, before the press conferences. After losing at home to Panathinaikos (1-0, goal from Olisadebe) in the first leg of the quarter-finals of the UEFA Cup in 2002-2003, Mourinho looked the other coach, Uruguayan Sergio Markarian, in the eye and said: "Don't start celebrating yet, because this tie is not over." Sure enough, Porto went to Greece and won 2-0 in extra time – the two goals from Derlei.

The following year, as he left the pitch after the draw with Deportivo da Corunha in the semi-final of the Champions League, he was at it again. He told the opposition coach, Maurio Silva: "We are going to win in Corunha." The Brazilian revealed what Mourinho had said just before the second leg, and FC Porto did win, 1-0, with a goal from Derlei.

At other times Mourinho kept his comments for the changing room, and they were solely for the ears of the team. In 2003, before a game with Benfica, Mourinho insisted on practising a tactic during training to counter the presence of the Croat Sokota up front for Benfica. When his players pointed out that the Benfica coach José Antonio Camacho usually played Zahovic and not

Sokota, he simply said: "That's when Camacho is winning. But this time he will be losing." The inference was that Porto would surely score first and Sokota would come on as a substitute.

Many journalists have been impressed by Mourinho's performance at press conferences and in other public appearances, and have no hesitation in being complimentary about him. In fact, when it suits him, Mourinho works hard to win them over.

The image Mourinho sought to portray was that of a loner, aloof and in control. But he also wanted to be admired, a bit of a dandy. He wore elegant clothes, bought a succession of expensive watches, and made a point of going to the hairdresser twice a week. He always maintained that he ate like a horse and took no care of his body at all, but the truth is that he has only put on eight pounds in 18 years. He never wears the same colours as his players, particularly during training sessions when photographers might picture them all together.

Mourinho says that he prefers not to stand out from the crowd. But he always wears clothes that make him do exactly that.

Mourinho's mother, Maria Júlia, said: "For a year now it's been my son who has taken all the pictures of me at home, simply so that I don't have to talk to the newspapers." Mourinho's gesture of putting all the photographs taken of him during childhood beyond possible public view is typical of the obsessive way he intended to manage his image. His father was the only person who was allowed to photograph him in private.

It is true that at one point Mourinho started to give interviews to magazines, with pictures of him beside his mother, or with one of his children on his lap. But those were in the days when he was in the wilderness, and it was important to seize every opportunity for publicity. It was desperately important to him not to be forgotten as he sought his place in the spotlight.

"When Robson and I went to Barcelona..." is literally what he said in one of those interviews, overlooking the rules of precedence between the chief coach and his assistant, in an evident attempt to make himself the focus of attention.

Today he no longer needs the publicity. Family members, friends, neighbours, even old colleagues, essentially most of the people who are relations or have relationships with him, keep mum when it comes to the man from Sétubal.

"When it comes to our personal relationship, all that gets told is what he says can be told," explains Carlos Mozer.

"We don't like people poking into our family life," is all mother Maria Júlia will say; she also refuses to be photographed and will only agree to talk by telephone. It is at least known that she works as a volunteer at a Catholic church in Sétubal.

Little more is known about Félix Mourinho, her husband, now in his late sixties. He follows his son's career on a daily basis, but does not watch the games on his doctor's advice. "My son has made me a very happy father" is all he will say, but he says it often.

The tabloids are strictly kept out of Mourinho's home, where Tami makes the rules. Mourinho says: "I virtually never lay down the law at home, and I virtually never row with my wife. As far as she and the children are concerned, my being famous counts for nothing."

His wife says: "Zé Mário never was much of a one for expressing his feelings, and I had to learn how to interpret what he wanted, by a gesture, an expression, or a look." But there is very little else Tami will say to cast any light on their more intimate relationship. They do not go to restaurants or act like a married couple in public in order to avoid the risk of unwanted publicity and intrusion into their personal lives.

His aunt Maria José Ulke said: "It annoys me

when, in interviews, they never talk about Mário Ledo [Mourinho's great uncle and the family benefactor] because they owe everything they are to him – as I do.

"They probably don't want to get mixed up with the politics, because Ledo was an important figure in Sétubal under the Salazar regime," she added. "Certainly Ledo was a right-wing figure whose politics would not be popular in Portugal today.

"But he doesn't deserve to be forgotten like that."

João Mário, José Mourinho's first cousin, is an exception when it comes to using fame by association to benefit a cause. Openly gay, a former drag queen and an interior decorator of some fame in Sétubal (and the subject of numerous articles in design magazines on a national level, in which he tends to leave out his family background), he says he has an excellent relationship with Mourinho, with occasional visits between the two branches of the family. At these, João Mário's partner, with whom he has lived for the last nine years, is treated in the same way by Mourinho as João treats Mourinho's wife.

"When I was a child we used to spend the holidays together. There is a certain age difference between us, and he sometimes used to make fun of me because of that, but today we have a very good relationship indeed. It's me who decorates their houses," says João Mário.

He adds that Mourinho and his wife like to live in sophisticated and relaxed surroundings. The furnishings are always approved by José Mourinho, to whom his wife sends pictures on his mobile.

"He never had anything negative to say about my views after I 'came out'. We've never talked about me being gay," said João Mário.

Following the death of his sister, José Mourinho is the sole heir to half of what remains of Mário Ledo's fortune. Even if he had never moved to Chelsea, he would be a wealthy man by Portuguese standards, and he always has been.

In Setúbal he recently bought what he regards as the home of his dreams, a beautiful property in Amoreiras with the Sierra da Arrabida mountains in the background, which he exchanged for the duplex next to the Bonfim Stadium. Replete with magnificent fireplace, security cameras, hydro-massage and sauna, this is the place he says he is setting aside for the day when he is unemployed again.

He says that it is Matilde ("Tami"), his wife, who makes all the important decisions in their family life. She was born in Angola in 1966 and is a former student of philosophy of the Catholic University, though she stopped a few steps short of taking her degree; it is she who runs the household and takes care of the children, overseeing their education and everyday life. It is said that, in the two-and-a-half years they lived in Oporto, she planned the creation of an aid foundation for needy children and that, when they were in Sétubal, she would pass on to staff the clothes the children had grown out of.

Mourinho studies football, does not watch much television, only listens to music in the car and, as a change, likes going to the cinema. But he has always enjoyed playing with his children.

"My greatest virtue, with apologies to other fathers, is that I'm the best father in the world," he once said, half as a joke and half seriously. Together, the four of them make up the classic nuclear family.

Mourinho denies he is rich, and is reckoned to be careful with his money. Certainly he is annoyed by the "absurd amounts" that he pays in tax. He says that he is 'a man of the right', politically.

"It is almost more difficult being on the right in Sétubal than being a person from Oporto in Lisbon," he jokes, but he holds up as one of his great political heroes the socialist Luís Felipe

Meneses. In any event, he always says that he "wants to laugh" whenever he sees a politician talking about football.

His aunt Maria José Ulke says sadly: "I haven't really talked to him since he got married. For a while I would meet them in downtown Sétubal, and they would ask how we were and make excuses about not coming to see us. But they lead a busy life, that's clear.

"He continues to be a favourite nephew, even though many people don't consider me to be part of the family now that I'm divorced," she adds.

On the streets of Sétubal and in the other places where he has lived, studied or worked over the years, there are now a lot of myths about José Mourinho. Some of these, the more innocent ones, are undoubtedly the result of word of mouth, with no evil intention: at the faculty, it is said somewhat impudently that he was better than Queiroz; at Estrela, he is compared unfavourably with Manuel Fernandes; at Leiria, he lent his apartment to the players to entertain their girlfriends.

Other rumours are clearly ill-intentioned: José Mourinho caused his sister a lot of grief; he often hits his wife; he refuses to lend his father the money needed for work on the house; when he was a boy, he used to do ballet; when his mother goes to the hairdresser she is full of praise for Portuguese football, but not a lot for her son. None of this is true. The only possible thing for the tabloids to pick up on was an upset at the beginning of 2004 involving a friend from childhood, Carlos Cardoso, which has since been resolved.

"Mourinho offered him tickets for the FC Porto-Corunha match, and their relationship started to improve," says a mutual acquaintance. "The town thinks a lot of José Mourinho. He is a great advert for Sétubal, although the fact of being with FC Porto will always upset some people," says Teodoro João, a journalist on the local newspaper *O Sétubalense* and a contemporary of Mourinho.

Tomé, a former colleague of Félix Mourinho and an old friend of the family, says: "People are jealous. They say nasty things about him because they don't know him. They don't like to see the boy next door making good. He is much more open than a lot of coaches. He's a great winner. He's someone special."

CHAPTER TEN
THE COACH ON THE COUCH

"As a leader, he has a kind of narcissism – and, basically, he's a leader because he believes that God has given him a special gift..."

CARLOS AMARAL DIA, psychiatrist

There was an awful lot of José Mourinho missing from the book by Luís Lourenço that bore his name and over which the Porto coach had full control. Notable by their absence were the entire family background, the opinions of other people and, above all, the explanation of the psychology of the man.

We had to search elsewhere to explain why he spoke to his players and to the press in a totally new way, performing mental somersaults to hold his audience in thrall. How he shook people awake and lifted the shutters on Portuguese football, a closed world that was traditionally stuffed with big shots, yes-men, and other, sometimes rather suspect, characters.

Some of those who fell out with him found him petulant, while others were immediately able to recognise someone who was exceptional, if given to idiosyncrasies.

Perhaps the most perceptive saw him as a human being who made his way in life by masking an almost pathological shyness with an air of arrogance; a man who tried to get the very best from what was available, and a man who always tried to get the maximum possible when it came to results.

"He was demanding, asked a lot of his players and was very aware of how to separate work and play," remembers Marques Pedrosa, former manager of Estrela da Armadora. "But we would fool about some of the time, too. When he was just out of college, for example, I would greet him with: 'Remember that these aren't school kids who come over here to play footie...' and he would make some joke in reply."

Journalist Luís Rojo remembers: "In the early days they said that he was gay and slept with Robson. But he handled that one well, and in an interview he said: "I'm not gay, and anyone can find that out by introducing me to their sister."

Carlos Mozer, assistant at Benfica, also has a personal contribution to make: "He doesn't get things mixed up. He doesn't have any difficulty in reconciling a serious approach with a sense of humour. He is extremely well adjusted when it comes to work."

For Carlos Amaral Dias, one of the best-known psychiatrists in Portugal, the personality of the man from Sétubal is a source of endless fascination, and something of a challenge.

"To tell the truth, José Mourinho exhibits two kinds of behaviour. One is the deadpan Mourinho, a man showing no emotion, no reaction, a side which is sometimes seen when he is on the pitch. The other side of him reveals an absolute certainty when it comes to getting his ideas across.

"He may appear to be arrogant, but this is a kind of thought-out leadership attitude, clearly with one face for the team and one for the outside. This is, in fact, a personality for which I have a great deal of admiration. Among the younger European coaches he is already regarded as an 'old pro'."

Rui Santos may not have the training of a psychiatrist, but he does identify a problem. What he finds disturbing is that, "Mourinho has an interesting rational side, but he has a partially paranoid side as well, which fluctuates between two complexes: grandeur and persecution.

"He is constantly swinging from hot to cold. He maintains a disconcerting silence when other people are jumping up and down, and gets all excited when they have stopped celebrating."

But even in this, psychiatrist Carlos Amaral Dias sees a strategy. It is a real temptation to put him on the psychiatrist's couch. As he explains: "What he succeeds in doing, above all, is to give people confidence in his own brand of leadership.

"There are three kinds of leader. There is the inspirational leader, who draws on emotional factors and who always places people ahead of numbers; there is the seductive leader, the populist, whose ideas transcend class distinctions and are linked with social justice; and there is the charismatic leader, who exudes a personal charisma in every move they make. Mourinho is clearly the charismatic type."

The psychiatrist then draws attention to the risks that leaders like Mourinho take when it comes to a crisis. "The problem with a charismatic leader is that, when the charisma runs out, there's nothing else left. This isn't a kind of leadership that is earned: he is a leader who to a certain extent is narcissistic. Basically, he's a leader because he is convinced that God has given him a certain gift.

"Time works against this kind of leader, and relationships with people of this kind deteriorate as time passes. Their fragility becomes apparent, their image starts to wear away, and the whole structure starts to change.

"I think Mourinho was right not to risk another year at FC Porto.

"On the other hand, to take a recent example, the problem of Carlos Queiroz at Real Madrid arose precisely because he did not possess that kind of charismatic leadership. What was needed there was a leader who would make the kind of changes which would have been good for the younger players – but were difficult to impose on established stars.

"Mourinho would certainly have been less afraid of the 'stars'. He would have been less susceptible to their influence, precisely because he is a narcissist, and he puts himself across as invincible. He believes he can do something, and this feeling is then transmitted to the person he is trying to convince."

José Peseiro, assistant to Queiroz at Madrid and subsequently taken on by Sporting as head coach, does not go along with this. "There are no infallible styles of leadership," he argues. "There are differences in the coaches at FC Porto, at Real Madrid, and at any other team.

"I'm not saying that Mourinho wouldn't have the capacity to coach Real, or any other top club. He is an intelligent man, with a lot of talent. But every coach has a different style of leadership depending on the context."

Rui Santos feels that Mourinho will find real challenges ahead. In his "Bible", Mourinho defends the idea of having cheap players on low salaries, without much experience. "It will be interesting to see how Mourinho gets on with a dressing room full of stars. That will be his baptism of fire. He has never worked in a hornet's nest, and having a bunch of stars together can be just that. Will he be able to turn their arrogance into obedience? We'll see."

Subsequent events at Stamford Bridge, where Mourinho not only assembled his 'bunch of stars' but then proceeded to win the Premier League by a country mile have more than answered Santos's doubts.

Luís Rojo, who continues to see Mourinho often, was expecting him to leave Porto as early as the beginning of 2004. After knocking Manchester United out of the Champions League,

José Mourinho became one of the most sought-after coaches in Europe, voted top in 2003 by in the UEFA website poll and third best by *World Soccer* magazine, after the Italians Carlo Ancelotti and Marcello Lippi.

At the same time Mourinho was starting to lift his own expectations higher and higher. "We're going to the final. I know it: we're going to the final," he told a friend from Lisbon on the day they eliminated United (1-1 at Old Trafford, after a 2-1 win in the first leg) according to an article on the Champions League in the magazine *Sabado*.

"I think he's cut out to be a manager in England, more than anything else," said Rojo. Octávio was surprised by the power Mourinho enjoyed at Porto. "When Pinto da Costa was in his prime, he would never have accepted being number two to a coach. Artur Jorge won everything, and so did Tomislav Ivic, and in both cases the chairman of FC Porto was on television saying that he wasn't worried when they left. Even when Pedroto died, Pinto da Costa said that he had only lost a friend and that basically the club would continue to prosper.

"Things have all changed now. He accepts being number two to Mourinho."

Rui Santos sees the reasoning behind events. "Mourinho had the ability to turn things on their head at FC Porto. Before him, everything began and ended with Pinto da Costa. Even some leading players, such as Vítor Baía or Jorge Costa, were considered more important than the coach."

Between 2001 and 2004, on the other hand, Porto was virtually a one-man club, with Mourinho at the helm. But the success he brought to the club actually strengthened Pinto de Costa's position as president.

"Pinto da Costa bowed down to the Mourinho dictatorship, but in the final analysis it was also good for him," is how Santos sums it up.

During the 2002-2003 season, Mourinho and Pinto da Costa were able to congratulate themselves on the fact that, during a period in which at least six other coaches and six other presidents had quit, they had won the national championship, the national cup and the European competition in which they were involved: what some people were already calling the football Grand Slam. Before the FC Porto of José Mourinho, only Celtic (1967-1968), Ajax (71-72), Gothenburg (81-82), PSV (87-88), Manchester United (98-99) and Galatasaray (99-00) had pulled this off.

In the book by Luís Lourenço, José Mourinho recalls a conversation with his wife in the car when, after winning the 2002-2003

Portuguese championship, they were driving through the streets of Oporto, with the celebrations in full swing.

"Look how the city's going crazy," Tami said to him.

"Yes, and this time I'm the one responsible for it," he replied.

CHAPTER ELEVEN
GOING IN PEACE?

"With Robson, many people saw him as simply along for the ride.

With Van Gaal, there was also a little antagonism.

But today everyone recognises that he is a great, great coach."

RAMON BESA, Journalist with *El Pais* (Spain)

It was clear to a lot of people that Mourinho would soon be leaving FC Porto. Top of the rumour league for a new destination was Chelsea, the English club acquired by Russian billionaire Roman Abramovich.

Despite investing heavily in players, his team, under the management of Italian coach Claudio

Ranieri had never quite succeeded in delivering the results. In April British newspapers reckoned the deal was definitely going to go through, and were talking about a contract worth £5 million.

Later there were reports that a decisive meeting between Mourinho and Abramovich had taken place in Corunha on 4 May, just before the second leg of the Champions League semi-final. *The Sunday Times* claimed that the meeting was held a day later, in London, where Mourinho, having already qualified for the final, went to watch the second leg of the semi-final between Chelsea and Monaco.

Regardless of the day when the deal was struck, the truth is that Mourinho had confided in his closest friends that he was heading for London. Pinto da Costa announced that he intended to complain to UEFA about the English club poaching his coach. Then the newspapers noticed that assistant coach Baltemar Brito had started going to special English classes . . .

Mourinho had said for a long time that he would stay with FC Porto if Pinto da Costa wanted him to, but now he changed his tune. "People aren't objective in the way they see things, and that's why it's impossible for me to be objective, especially now with so many big games coming up," he said before the match in Corunha.

Maniche, one of his star players, soon made it clear that he was prepared to follow Mourinho, the man who had plucked him from the Benfica reserve team and turned him into one of the best midfield players in Europe. Mariche said: "Of course I would like to continue working with him. He's one of the best in the world.

"It's true that I'm under contract to FC Porto for two more years, and we are already working on a new deal But if an offer comes along that looks good for everyone, then I'm prepared to consider it. And in that case, to go to a club where Mourinho was in charge would be the icing on the cake."

Around that time, Mourinho was already saying openly that, "Maniche is only great because he was coached by me," but acknowledging that, "he doesn't try to make things complicated, he makes them easier. For me, that's a talent, because he's a player who can play at the same tempo for 90 minutes."

Mourinho's departure from Porto had started to look likely as early as January when, following a draw at Alvalade, he made the comment: "I don't like Portuguese football because it doesn't like me." The fact that Portugal was "a small country" made him sad, and the expression 'Far away, far away, far away!' had become some kind of mantra.

Ten days earlier the *Jornal de Notícias* had published an interview in which he announced that he had already registered his son with a primary school in Oporto for the year 2004-2005, giving this assurance: "If the president [Pinto da Costa] says 'don't go', then I won't go."

Mourinho was involved in more controversy after a match against Sporting, who had equalised while one of the Porto players (João Vieira Pinto) was being treated for an apparently serious injury. Mourinho was furious with the referee and with the Sporting players. After the final whistle he was involved in an incident in the tunnel with Sporting midfielder Rui Jorge, whose shirt was torn. Later, after his move to Chelsea, he was fined £2,000 and banned for 10 days by the Portuguese FA.

Rui Santos says: "José Mourinho was much closer to leaving than he was letting on. It was very clearly what he wanted. The wheel had come full circle, and he had his sights set on other things. In that context, the Apito Dourado affair [a corruption case in which, according to the newspaper *Expresso*, Pinto da Costa was to be investigated by the police] was the pretext he needed. It wasn't clear what ramifications the affair would have on FC Porto, or whether the image of Portuguese football would be tarnished."

If the Chelsea deal failed to materialise,

Mourinho was still a target for Liverpool and Spurs in England and, quite possibly, for both Real Madrid and his old club Barcelona.

Luís Rojo said at the time: "The Barcelona fans would like to see him back, but now as the main coach. The Spanish press has written a lot about his success in Portugal, but the wins were always Mourinho's wins, never FC Porto's."

Mourinho had talked about "three English clubs and another three Italian" as the ones that interested him most, and never mentioned Spain in the same context, even though, in the past, he had many times said that he would "love" to go back to Barcelona (he said the same thing about Benfica).

At the end of March, Octávio Machado was worried about how things would pan out at Porto. He said: "Apart from Fernando Santos, no trainer has ever lasted more than two years at FC Porto. And now Pinto da Costa is desperately trying to hold on to Mourinho for a fourth consecutive year. It is going to be painful... the coach leaving is going to tear an enormous hole in the club.

"There will be nothing after Mourinho. Pinto da Costa is worn out, and he's no longer the safe bet for the future that he once was. Seriously, I am curious to see how this all turns out."

No further clues about the future emerged as FC Porto approached the last stage of the Champions League. In April, Mourinho's prestige was already enormous, regardless of whether or not Porto went on to win the domestic or European titles.

And when he finally did quit Portugal, though Mourinho left behind him some acrimony, it seems that most of the people he had fallen out with had subsequently forgiven him.

"We are friends," is all Barbosa will say today. Diamantino Miranda, who, when he was being coached by Mourinho, had accused him of "acting in bad faith and displaying a lack of intelligence" has also come round. "Today I understand his attitude. I also realise he has always acted that way, and enjoyed great success," he says.

Even Ramon Besa, a journalist with *El País* in Barcelona and one of the most ferocious critics of the Robson/Mourinho partnership in 1996-97, now speaks of Mourinho with admiration. "With Robson, many people saw Mourinho as simply along for the ride. With Van Gaal there was also a little antagonism. With Van Gaal, it's Van Gaal who gives the orders, and that's it. But today everyone recognises that Mourinho is a great, great coach," said the Spaniard, who has since apologised publicly to both Robson and Mourinho.

At Antas, the feeling of resentment about him leaving would only be temporary, according to Mourinho. He said: "Whether they like it or not, I am going to be recognised as a coach who shaped the history of FC Porto." When everyone connected with the club looked back in 10 years' time they would cheer him and make him welcome, Mourinho promised before winning the final of the Champions League, already aware that going to Chelsea was going to cause some ructions.

There are only two people who still make no secret of their dislike for Mourinho: Octávio Machado, and Martin O'Neill, the former Celtic manager, whose team lost to Porto in the final of the UEFA Cup in 2003. O'Neill cannot forgive Mourinho for the "excessively harsh" criticism of Celtic's performance in that decisive match, and in various interviews he has accused Mourinho of spending the whole of the 2002-2004 period ordering his players, in particular Carlos Alberto, to take dives so as to win free kicks.

Octávio Machado, for his part, maintains that, despite the clashes in the past between the FC Porto coach and a number of other Portuguese coaches, most of them had a grudging admiration for the man from Sétubal and were pleased with his successes in Europe, even if they would like to see "a different attitude."

"I've got nothing against him personally," Octávio said. "He never beat me. Not with Sporting when I was at FC Porto, nor at FC Porto when I was with Sporting; and, obviously, not with Leiria when I was at FC Porto. With Sporting, when he was an assistant to Robson, I beat him twice in a fortnight, something that prompted their departure from Antas," he remembers.

Sabry continued to loathe Mourinho deeply until the FC Porto-Estrela da Amadora match in 2003-2004, when the coach turned to him and gave him a hug, admitting that he had been "too harsh" during an outburst at Benfica. Blame for the more outspoken of the interviews always rests with one of two people: the journalist who is conducting the interview, or the person who is giving it.

Both Sabry and Mourinho agree that the journalist was to blame.

CHAPTER TWELVE
VICTORY AND THREATS

"In four days I was approached by eight different agents who said they had been instructed by Mr Abramovich to negotiate with me. One because he was a friend of his, one because he was a friend of the chairman, another one because they spoke the same language, another one because he lives in London, and another one because he has a boat moored next to his..."

JOSE MOURINHO

The story of Mourinho's last days at FC Porto could have been a tale of a glorious triumph in the Champions League. It was not – at least, not exactly. Because of the importance that Pinto da Costa attached to his coach, the rift between him and Mourinho would never be healed.

Two other factors helped exacerbate the situation. Being aware that Mourinho was going to be worth his weight in gold in an international context, all the FIFA agents, would-be agents and other money-grabbers who habitually gravitate towards the football world, mobilised to make sure they got their share of the bounty.

"In four days I was approached by eight different agents who said they had been instructed by Mr Abramovich to negotiate with me. One because he was a friend of his, one because he was a friend of the chairman, another one because they spoke the same language, another one because he lives in London, and another one because he has a boat moored next to his..." said Mourinho, who by that time was already in London, ready to sign with Chelsea just one week after FC Porto won the Champions League.

Being a commercial asset was just part of the problem. He was becoming trapped between those who were out to make money from his departure and those who wanted to save face by getting him to stay.

Mourinho was also touched by personal scandal that had been stirred up by the tabloids. There was supposed to have been an extra-marital flirtation, or even a love affair, and the woman was said to have been the wife or mistress of an important person at Porto. Juiciest of all, the mystery woman was rumoured to be the wife of one of the FC Porto players in the process of a divorce.

But nothing was proved, nobody was named and Mourinho immediately made it known that *VIP*, the magazine that was responsible for the first rumour, would be sued. Just as predicted, he would not leave Portugal in peace.

Porto reached the final of the Champions League after defeating Deportivo at Corunha, a team that had not had a goal scored against them at home throughout the tournament. The Spaniards had beaten such heavyweights as AC Milan 4-0 shortly before, and were hot favourites to go through to the final in Gelsenkirchen, Germany, after drawing the first leg at Porto 0-0.

But Mourinho's team saw off a determined opening burst from Deportivo and ended up winning by a single goal. At the moment they scored, the trainer took a risk that was rare for someone who, most of the time, refuses to place control of his destiny in anyone else's hands: he put all his trust in Derlei, the player to whom he owed so much and who had caused him so much worry for so long.

Injured in the first half of the season, the Brazilian whom Mourinho had discovered at

Leiria and turned into one of the most sought-after strikers in European football, had rejoined the team a few weeks before, speeding up his recovery precisely with the Deportivo game in mind. It had to be Derlei who scored the decisive goal.

Even short of his best form, even when physically and mentally exhausted, Derlei did not let Mourinho down. And score he did, from the penalty spot. The end of the game was ragged, tense, nervous – but FC Porto came through to win 1-0.

Their pride wounded by the tenacity of the Portuguese team, the Spanish press were divided between complimenting Mourinho and his players and jeering at them. The most critical of the Spaniards called the team "hard cases", and blamed the coach.

"They say that Gelsenkirchen is cold and flat. It's the perfect place for FC Porto to take on Europe with their brand of anti-football," wrote one journalist.

"It's FC Porto, the monster that UEFA created," said Julián Ruiz, a journalist with *Marca*. Mourinho's team, meanwhile, had just kept on winning when least expected and riding their luck. They had almost gone out to Manchester United earlier in the competition, when United claimed that Paul Scholes had a goal wrongly disallowed, and they could just as easily have conceded a penalty at Corunha as gaining one. But in the history of football, goals have never been re-instated or penalties awarded after the game is over.

Porto had won the right to compete in the final of the most important club competition in world football. The game was coming at the perfect time, as Mourinho's team had already clinched the Portuguese championship, finally seeing off Sporting and Benfica. Now they could concentrate exclusively on the Champions League.

The Portuguese Cup final, for which they had also qualified in the meantime, assumed a low priority in the minds of the players and of Mourinho as well, and they lost rather ingloriously. After two league championships, one UEFA Cup, and one Portuguese Cup in two seasons, Mourinho's team simply could not find the motivation to overcome a Benfica side fighting to give their great mass of fans their first trophy after eight years in the wilderness.

Porto went ahead with a goal from Derlei, now fully recovered from injury, but Benfica equalised through the Greek Fyssas, and, in extra time, Simoa Sabrosa headed the winner. José Mourinho made his opinion plain after the match: if Porto played with the same lack of will to win in the Champions League final, they would lose again.

But on 26 May at Gelsenkirchen, which had warmed to the prospect of the final, this prophecy did not come true. It was clear that this was the last, great challenge Mourinho would face at Porto, and he was determined to bow out on a high note. He was now being pursued by English, Italian and Spanish clubs – Real Madrid, Barcelona, Liverpool and Tottenham were among those interested, though none of them was ever likely to get ahead of Chelsea in the race to sign him – and, in the week before the final, Mourinho really sparkled.

He surprised journalists at press conferences by answering questions in Portuguese or Spanish, in English or Italian, and even in somewhat hesitant French or Catalan (only German still eluded him). The fans were enthusiastic and the journalists gave him compliments such as "the most sought-after coach in Europe", shaping the general impression that this would be his last game with FC Porto.

Their opponents in the final were Monaco, led by another outstanding young coach, the Frenchman Didier Deschamps.

The French started the game well but Porto took the lead against the run of play through Carlos Alberto's goal just before half-time, and in the second half, the Portuguese team started to steamroller their opponents. Deco made it 2-0 with a magic finish in the closing minutes of an extraordinary game and then the Russian Aleichev added a third.

A few minutes later, while the players were still celebrating on the pitch, the officials jubilant in the stands and, for a while at least, the whole world seemed to be Porto fans, the most surprising thing was to see Mourinho, standing poker-faced at first, showing no emotion. He grabbed his children, kissing them in public, and then finally stood alone again, his players having long gone off to celebrate, looking for all the world as if he had no part in this at all.

Later on, Mourinho would say that his lack of reaction was due to the fact that the game had been decided much earlier, at least 15 to 20 minutes before the final whistle, and that he had therefore had time to compose himself. It was a way of showing off, this passivity.

Mourinho had succeeded in achieving the Holy Grail of the Champions League against all the odds, and yet he did not join in the festivities on the pitch, or the night after, when the team joined the convoys that inundated the city of Oporto until the early hours, flags and banners waving, and the police escorting them through.

It could have been a chastisement, a way of punishing the country for the lack of enthusiasm with which Mourinho believed it had greeted the Porto's victory at Corunha weeks before.

It could have been weakness, something that might have suddenly afflicted Mourinho after a highly stressful period, with Maniche picking up a drink-driving charge a few days before the final of the Champions League perhaps being the last straw.

It could have been been weariness, pain, badly expressed joy; it could have been a thousand things.

But the main reason behind the absence of celebrations was fear over threats made to Mourinho's family. Mourinho has talked about this since moving to London. A lunatic fringe at Porto had threatened his wife and children, leaving him worried and unable to fully join in the celebrations after the final whistle of the Champions League final.

The story, which, at the time, appeared in the magazine *O Crime*, even went as far as to suggest that someone had been planted on the plane flying Porto to the Champions League Final in Germany with the intention of approaching and unsettling Mourinho. The inference was that Mourinho's alleged affair was the reason that threats were made. And while that may be pure fiction, the threats themselves were real enough, as Mourino would later confirm.

It was because of the threats that, it is claimed, Mourinho's family abandoned the terrace for the access tunnel. And it was because of this that, on arriving in Portugal, José Mourinho immediately set out for Lisbon with his wife and children, escaping from the celebrations in Oporto.

The true story will probably never be told. Between the information and misinformation it is very difficult to distinguish what really happened and what, on the other hand, was simply invented so as to draw attention away from something else or to satisfy personal vendettas.

But the fact that the threats were real can be taken from Mourinho's own words: "I was too concerned for my family to take part in the celebrations". He said that he felt "obliged" to "change his personal and social life" in response to the threats.

CHAPTER THIRTEEN
THE SPECIAL ONE

"I believe that I'm special"

JOSÉ MOURINHO

The press conference that introduced José Mourinho as the new Chelsea manager, held on 2 June 2004, was broadcast live by SKY News and CNN, which gives some idea of how far the young man from Sétubal had come in his profession after just four years as a coach.

Peter Kenyon, Chelsea's chief executive, made a simple introduction: "I am pleased to present José Mourinho as the new Chelsea manager" but, after praising the work of Claudio Ranieri, predecessor to Mourinho, and finding himself obliged to justify the change, Kenyon added: "He is the best manager in Europe."

In somewhat stilted but grammatically correct

English, Mourinho thanked him, and then spoke about the threats that had been made against his family from the lunatic fringe that resented him leaving Porto, expressing his sadness about the grudges that some people bore against him. He announced that he would be joined at Stamford Bridge by the physio Rui Faria, assistant trainer Baltemar Brito, goalkeeper trainer Silvino Louro, opposition observer André Villas Boas and press liaison man Eládio Paramés, who, despite not having worked with Mourinho at FC Porto, was largely responsible for persuading Vale e Azevedo to offer him a deal with Benfica in 2000.

And then, for the first time in many weeks, José Mourinho smiled. The pictures went round the world: Mourinho was smiling, his friends were with him, and everything was all right again. After the congratulations came the serious stuff. When British journalists asked him whether his first objective for the team was to win the Premiership, the new Chelsea manager had a rather flat reply for them: "The first objective is to win the first game, on 14 August".When they asked him about his second objective, it was Mr Deadpan again: "Winning the second, on 21 August." He wished FC Porto success and promised loyalty to his old club: "If we meet in the Champions League, it will be the only time I want them to lose."

As far as Chelsea was concerned, his comment: "It is the perfect club for my ambitions" certainly didn't indicate that he was intimidated by the Stamford Bridge set-up. Describing his own attitude, he was extremely candid: "I don't call myself arrogant. I'm not one of those coaches who never wins. I am a European champion. I believe that I'm special."

The negotiating process had not been easy. It had started in March, just after FC Porto under Mourinho had knocked Manchester United out of the Champions League. There were all sorts of rumours flying about over Mourinho's future. Some of the offers were real, some imaginary. Some of the speculation was laughable, such as the story run in the *News of the World* which claimed Louis Van Gaal, Mourinho's former boss at Barcelona, was ready to leave Ajax and join Chelsea as Mourinho's number two.

The Chelsea deal had been on the cards for a long time, although at that first press conference at Stamford Bridge, Mourinho said that the initial contact from Chelsea had come a few days before the Champions League final, there are claims that he and Abramovitch had met much earlier, in early March.

When he was in London to see Chelsea play Monaco in the Champions League's other semi-final, Mourinho took his wife Tami along to see the city, look round for a house and find a school for the children.

Mourinho was anxious not to prejudice Porto's chances of an historic win, so negotiations were restricted to a circle of just four people: Peter Kenyon, Jorge Mendes, José Mourinho and Israeli Pini Zahevi, a FIFA agent.

Chelsea's existing manager, Claudio Ranieri, was paid off with £6 million, enough, Kenyon hoped, to head off any public relations difficulties that might follow. The charming and highly quotable Italian, who had been very successful at Valencia previously, was particularly popular.

So Chelsea finally set about securing the services of "the most wanted man in Europe" as *The Guardian* described him. And Mourinho, who had already said earlier that he was only in Portugal because of his wife and children – "football is the same the world over", as he put it – finally achieved what he had wanted for so long: working with one of the top clubs in England in the role of manager (and not simply "coach"), which would allow him to control many more areas of the club than would have been the case in Portuguese football, even for Mourinho himself at Porto.

Chelsea had been bought in June 2003 by Russian billionaire Roman Abramovich. The club won nothing the following season. They had reached the semi-finals of the Champions League and were runner-up to Arsenal in the Premiership. The first challenge for Mourinho was to make sure this experience was not repeated, and Abramovitch, in the style of Florentino Perez (Real Madrid) or Silvio Berlusconi (AC Milan), soon showed that he was ready to invest as much as was necessary.

Abramovich, 37, dubbed the "tsar of football", had a fascinating background as a self-made man. He was orphaned at the age of three, and two decades later had built a small business empire based on an initial investment in rubber ducks for children. Born in the river port of Saratov in Southern Russia, Roman lost his mother to septicaemia when he was only 18 months old, and his father in a civil engineering accident just 18 months later. He grew up in Siberia, where he was looked after by an uncle who was employed in the oil industry.

His rise was meteoric: shy and rather bucolic-looking, the young Russian had first worked at the Gubkin Institute and in a gas company in Moscow, made an investment in the toy factory, acquired a share in Runicom, a multinational dealing in raw materials, and become an associate of Russian television baron Boris Berezovsky (in

1992), buying with him Sidneft, an oil company that thrived in the wave of privatisations in the post-socialist period. He became a friend of Vladimir Putin, the Russian premier, was elected to the Duma, the Russian parliament, and became governor of the province of Chukotka. He became boss of Rusal, an aluminium company, bought and later sold a quarter of Aeroflot, the Russian airline, bought the Russian ice-hockey team Avangarde Omsk, secured interests in the food industry and in pharmaceuticals, and, by the time he came to the United Kingdom by way of the automobile industry, had a fortune estimated at £6,000 million, making him the second richest man in Russia and the 25th richest person in the world.

Married and with five children, it is said that Roman Abramovich tries to live the simple life. He does not smoke or drink, wears jeans, lets his beard grow, has a passion for pizzas and keeps his family out of the limelight, driving around in cars with blacked-out windows and surrounded by bodyguards – even, it is said, when in the bathroom. A simple life, or simply incredible: he has luxury properties in St Tropez, England and Russia, including a hundred-acre property in Moscow. He has three luxury yachts (two of them turned up, sparkling, off the Algarve coast during Euro 2004), a number of helicopters, a private jet and even an airliner. Accused of having 'dangerous relationships' with Putin and other key Russian political and economic figures, he has been caught up in a number of corruption scandals – and has emerged without a stain on his reputation every time.

Abramovitch's passion: football. First he tried to buy Manchester United, but his bid failed. Then he bought Chelsea, took on Peter Kenyon from United, and spent more than £200 million on the club, securing the likes of Sebastien Véron, Hernan Crespo, Claude Makelele and Wayne Bridge. He put his trust in Claudio Ranieri to create what he hoped would be the best team in the world.

But eventually Abramovitch had come to the conclusion that money alone would not do it. He needed the man he considered the best coach in the world – Mourinho, who had put a winning team together for less than £30 million.

Mourinho says that he co-ordinates a football team the way someone plays chess, thinking not only about the next move but the four that will follow it. Certainly, he appears to think of everything. He has even been known to train with only 10 players, trying out a 4-3-2 system, so as to be prepared for having a man sent off. Other people have been fascinated by his maxim that says the opponent is an enemy who he really hates.

And, by eight o'clock in the morning, it is not unusual for him to have absorbed the lessons to be learned from a game the previous evening, having already watched the video.

In England, plenty of people had their doubts. In an article published in the *Daily Mail*, journalist David Jones accused him of "lack of feeling for the players" and an "obsession about hiding his past." In *The Sunday Times*, Ian Hawkey praised him for having "declared an embargo on false modesty", but was sarcastic about the press conference at which, in the aftermath of the Corunha game, the Portuguese trainer told in detail of how every single one of his tactical forecasts had come true.

Denis Campbell, in *The Observer*, called Mourinho "intense, ambitious, and complicated", described him as being an "abrasive and confident figure" and identified his method as being "my way or no way" – Mourinho's personality has been generally analysed as that of a "control freak". *The Observer* called the Portuguese championship "one of the most modest leagues in Europe", using this to justify its reservations about Mourinho. Even so, the newspaper quoted the forward Benni McCarthy, who identified Mourinho as "the best coach in Europe and the world" and asserted that he would "lead well", with a galaxy of stars. And that, the newspaper concluded, taking account of all the differences that have divided the coach and player in the past, was really saying something.

Reading the many interviews given by Bobby Robson about Mourinho's move to Chelsea, this stands out: "Winning in Europe is easier than winning in the Premiership," he repeatedly said. "Mourinho is entering an area which he doesn't know. He is going to come up against a league that is very different to the Portuguese situation. He's going to compete with the greats. On five or six occasions, during European matches, he has beaten some great teams. In England he will have to do it 38 times."

Mourinho, who said of Robson: "He is like a father to me, and everything I win will be dedicated to him", soon showed his old mentor that what he could do in Portugal, he could do in England, too. Chelsea lost just one of their 38 games in the Premier league in 2004-2005 and finished as champions, 12 points ahead of Arsenal.

Porto may have lost a coach, but they gained a great deal from Mourinho's time in charge, not least a cash bonanza from their successes in Europe. And they cashed in again when Mourinho returned to sign Carvalho and Ferreira.

Among Portuguese coaches, the departure of the man from Sétubal resulted in a consensus of opinion that is rarely seen. In a survey conducted by Correio da Manha some of his most vociferous detractors in the past had only positive things to say about the departure of the FC Porto trainer. In reply to the question: "Is Mourinho among the top Portuguese coaches of all time?", Toni, José Couceiro, Jesualdo Ferreira, Artur Jorge, Jorge Jesus, Manuel Fernandes and Vitor Pontes were absolutely in agreement: "Yes".

All of them, incidentally, used the expression "the best".

CHRONOLOGY

1963-68: José Mário dos Santos Mourinho Félix is born in Sétubal, Portugal, on 26th January 1963, and lives his first five years in the semi-aristocratic environment of Mário Ascensao Ledo's family. Mário Ledo was a great-uncle from his mother side and a great conservative industrialist from Sétubal. The family lives on a pleasant estate at Freguesia dos Aires, near Palmela, and enjoys the fruits of prosperity under the political regime of Oliveira Salazar. Young José Mourinho grows up loving sport, especially football; his father is a professional goalkeeper, having played for Vitória de Sétubal, Benelenses and the national team.

1968-78: José Mourinho, his father (Félix Mourinho), his mother (Maria Júlia) and his sister (Teresa), moved to Bairro do Montalvao in

Setubal. Mourinho is sent to elite schools, and is noticed for his restraint and leadership among a very loud group of friends who all love five-a-side tournaments. Plays football as a student, but doesn't seem to have enough technique to move towards a career as a professional.

1978-81: As the son of a football coach, José Mourinho divides his time between the school, the junior training team session at Benelenses, and the houses and restaurants where the players coached by his father get together. Thinking of becoming a coach himself, he learns the basics from his father and helps him out by observing opposing teams, writing reports, carrying messages to professional footballers and organizing the ball boys.

1981-87: In a final attempt to become a professional footballer, Mourinho joins Rio Ave, coached by his father, but never starts a game for the first team. He starts taking a degree in business management but lasts only one day. He now commits himself to being a professional coach. Enrols for a physical education degree at ISEF, [Higher Institute of Physical Education]. Still plays football as a semi-professional (and sometimes an amateur) for Benelenses (second division), Sesimbra and finally at Comercio and Industria.

1987-90: Completes his degree and starts teaching PE at secondary schools in Sétubal, at the same time teaching children with special needs. Becomes engaged to Matilde, the girl he has been going out with since he was 17. Gets his first position as a coach (Vitória de Sétubal junior team). His career gets underway.

1990-92: José Mourinho gets the job of assistant coach at Estrela da Amadora thanks to his friend, the Amadora coach Manuel Fernandes. He quickly makes his mark with both his technical ability and his dedication to work. The pair are fired before the end of the first season. Mourinho returns to the Vitória juniors. Manuel Fernandes makes a promise that they will work together again one day.

1992-93: Through Manuel Fernandes, Mourinho meets Bobby Robson, who persuades Souza Cintra to hire him as English translator at Sporting Lisbon. So begins a long professional relationship and friendship with the British coaching legend. When the trio is fired due to bad results, it is Mourinho – not Fernandes, the real assistant coach – who is invited to by Robson to join him in his next post.

1993-96: Hired as an assistant to Bobby Robson at FC Porto, José Mourinho is in a battle for the number two position. In the end, it is Mourinho who is closest to Robson's heart. After a winning run, Robson is hired by the Barcelona – and with him goes José Mourinho.

1996-97: At Barcelona, Robson and Mourinho inherit a team with some of the greatest players in the world (Ronaldo, Stoichkov, Kluivert, Luís Figo and Guardiola, among many others). The pair quickly change the team's strategy, and the captain, causing waves at the club. Chairman Josep Lluiz Nuñez has been dreaming for two years of hiring the Dutchman Louis Van Gaal, and even after winning two trophies, Robson goes to PSV Eindhoven at the end of only one season. Mourinho stays, but in a subordinate position.

1997-2000: José Mourinho proves his competence to the demanding Van Gaal by giving excellent reports on opposing teams and watching out for undiscovered talent from minor clubs. Little by little he climbs the hierachy. Mourinho begins to think about moving back to Portugal in 1999, but keeps winning titles. He is frequently to be seen in the stand at the Nou Camp, getting a bird's eye view of the game and sending messages by mobile to Van Gaal.

2000-01: Barcelona's new coach, Serra Ferrer, doesn't include Mourinho in his plans, and the Portuguese decides this is the time to strike out for a coaching job of his own. He returns to Portugal – refusing an invitation to be Bobby Robson's assistant at Newcastle – and sends out word that he is available. Finishes the famous Powerpoint presentation that he calls "The Bible" – it contains all his thoughts about tactics and training. Invited to Benfica. Stays for only two months but he is missed still. Mourinho reckons he has a chance of the job at Sporting, but it doesn't come off.

2001-02: After a period of unemployment filled with promises that never came true, José Mourinho finds himself at the position of having to accept a more modest offer and signs up with Uniao de Leiria. Has tussles with players and management, but brings the team success. Discovers (or re-discovers) players such as Derlei, Nuno Valente, Tiago, Silas, Maciel – most will follow him later to FC Porto.

2002-03: Hired by FC Porto during a difficult separation between the club and coach Octávio Machado. José Mourinho promises at the very beginning that Porto will be champions next season. Begins to shape his ideal team, with some players hired from Uniao de Leiria and from the Sétubal region.

2003: Absolute success, as promised. Mourinho wins the championship with FC Porto, the Portuguese Cup and – the biggest feat – the UEFA Cup. Becomes one of the hottest coaching properties in football.

2004: Approached by some of the main European clubs, he repeats the feat of winning the domestic championship and a European competition – this time the biggest prize of all, the Champions League – taking FC Porto to the peak of European football. His relationship with the club's hierachy, particularly with the chairman, Pinto da Costa, starts to deteriorate. He finally gets to point of thinking that going abroad is a concrete possibility – and the future brings him to Chelsea, now owned by the Russian billionaire Roman Abramovich.

2005: Takes the British press and public by storm as he wins the Premiership with Chelsea by a mile.

BIBLIOGRAPHY

ASSUNÇÃO, Manuel, 'Chelsea covets half of FC Porto', *Público*, Lisbon, 8th May, 2004, 1.
'Spanish press has criticised Collina and the style of FC Porto', *Público*, Lisbon, 6th May, 2004, 1.

BARBOSA, Nuno; SOUSA, Rui, 'Tomorrow negotiations begin for Deco', *Record*, Lisbon, 13th June, 2004, 1.
'Ricardo is besieged', *Record*, Lisbon, 13th June, 2004, 1.

BARROSO, Eduardo, *Confessions of a Sporting fan*, 1st edition, Lisbon: Oficina do Livro – Sociedade Editorial Lda., 2001. 216 pp.

BERNARDINO, Carla; ABREU, Paulo; AIDO, Paulo; BRÁS, Rui, 'All Mourinho's secrets', *TV Guia*, Lisbon, 1st June, 2004, 4.

BÖLÖNI, Laszlo, *Laszlo Bölöni's notepad*, 1st edition, Lisbon: Booktree – Sociedade Editorial Lda., 2002. 190 pp.

BREDA, Rui, 'Mourinho centenary', *Doze*, Lisbon, 20th February, 2004, 4.

CAETANO, Filipe, 'Troubled hiring', *Mais Futebol* (www.maisfutebol.iol.pt) (consulted on 30th March, 2004).

CALHAU, Pedro, 'This isn't Paok', *24 Horas*, Lisbon, 12th November, 2000, 1.

CAMPBELL, Denis, 'Luxury coach', *The Observer*, London, 30th May, 2004, 1.

CAMPOS, Mário David, 'What force is this?', *Visão*, Oeiras, 18th March, 2004, 2.

CORREIA, Augusto, 'I no longer want to be a run-of-the-mill manager', *Jornal de Notícias*, Porto, 6th February, 1999, 1.

CRUZ, Carlos, 'Who tricked the manager?', *Record*, Lisbon, 20th December, 2000, 1.

CURADO, Paulo, 'Real Madrid prefers Ricardo Carvalho to Luisão', *Público*, Lisbon, 22nd June, 2004, 1.

DEUSDADO, Daniel, '8th highest-paid in Europe', *Expresso*, Oeiras, 5th June, 2004, 2.

ESTEVES, Rui, 'I want to return to Benfica', *A Capital*, Lisbon, 20th March, 2001, 2.

FARIA, Álvaro; PEREIRA, Fernando, 'Fights with FC Porto excited Mourinho', *Jornal de Notícias*, Porto, 19th March, 2000, 1.

FERNANDES, Ferreira, 'Team practice sessions? Only if there's dosh in it', *Correio da Manhã*, Lisbon, 8th June, 2004, 1.

FERREIRA, Abílio, 'A manager who annoys the class', *Expresso*, Oeiras, 19th January, 2002, 1.

FERREIRA, GOMES, 'Vilarinho is no longer in charge', *Record*, Lisbon, 15th December, 2000, 5.

FERREIRA, Paula Santos, 'The refuge of the "hero"', *TV 7 Dias*, Sintra, 1st June, 2004, 1.

FIDÉLIS, Amílcar, 'Managing Benfica was unforgettable...', *Correio da Manhã* (Sunday Magazine), Lisbon, 26th August, 2001, 4.

FIEL, Jorge, 'Mourinho's 7 secrets', *Expresso* (Única), Oeiras, 22nd May, 2004, 8.

FILIPE, Luís, 'From translator to manager', *O Independente*, Lisbon, 22nd September, 2000, 1.

FONSECA, Pedro Prostes da, 'José Mourinho introduces his family', *Nova Gente*, Queluz, 1st January, 1997, 4.

FRANCISCO, Luís, 'There were no retaliations', *Público*, Lisbon, 28th July, 2000, 1.

FRIAS, Rui, 'Between insult and forgiveness', *Diário de Notícias*, Lisbon, 6th May, 2004, 1.
'Mourinho on a par with Eusébio', *Diário de Notícias*, Lisbon, 27th April, 2004, 1.

GALEANO, Eduardo, *The Book of Embraces*, 9th edition, Porto Alegre, L & PM Editores 2002, 272 pp.

G., S., 'José Mourinho, the superstar manager', *L'Humanité* (www.humanite.fr) (consulted on 23rd April, 2004).

GUTÍERREZ, José Ramón Fernández, 'One plays football the way one lives....', *TV Azteca* (www.tvazteca.com) (consulted on 6th June, 2004).

HAWKEY, Ian, 'The Commander Mourinho', *The Sunday Times*, London, 9th May, 2004, 2.

JONES, David, 'Demons that are driving Mourinho', Daily Mail, London, 28th May, 2004, 2.

LAWTON, Matt; CURRY, Steve, 'What a farce!', *Daily Mail*, London, 28th May, 2004, 2

LEITE, Augusto, 'Mourinho at Chelsea', *Record*, Lisbon, 23rd April, 2004, 1.

LOPES, João, 'Mourinho punished', *Record*, Lisbon, 15th June, 2004, 1.

LOURENÇO, Luís, *José Mourinho*, 7th edition, Lisbon, Prime Books – Sociedade Editorial Lda., 2003, 190 pp.

MAGALHÃES, Júlio; PINTO, Marcos, 'Love conquered all', *TV 7 Dias*, Sintra, 1st June, 2004, 3.

MANHA, João Querido, 'Double harvests', *Doze*, Lisbon, 16th January, 2004, 5.

MARÍAS, Javier, *Wild ones and sentimental ones*, 1st edition, Lisbon, Publicações Dom Quixote, 2000, 184 pp.

MIGUÉNS, Alberto, 'New mentality', *Benfica*, Lisbon, 5th December, 2001, 1.

MÓNICA, Maria Filomena, 'Mourinho's statuesque knees', *Público*, Lisbon, 19th June, 2004, 1.

MOURINHO, José, 'Barcelona doesn't cry over Figo', *MaisFutebol* (www.maisfutebol.iol.pt) (consulted on 30th March, 2004).
'Back to Portugal', *MaisFutebol* (www.maisfutebol.iol.pt) (consulted on 30th March, 2004).

MOUTINHO, Evelise, 'I want to dedicate this cup to my family and everyone who likes me', *Lux*, Lisbon, 28th May, 2004, 3.

NOGUEIRA, Carlos, 'Journey to Mourinho's land', *24 Horas*, Lisbon, 27th April, 2004, 2.

NUNES, Miguel Costa, 'Money's not enough to put the brake on Porto', *Sábado*, Lisbon, 7th May, 2004, 2.

OLIVEIRA, Paulo, 'The war that spoilt the party', *Tal & Qual*, Lisbon, 4th June, 2004, 2.

ÓSCAR, Luís (compiler), *Fiftieth Anniversary Record Book*, 1st edition, Lisbon, Asa Editores, 1999, 594 pp. (2 volumes).

OSTERMANN, Rui Carlos, *The road to rout – Story of five world cups without Pelé*, 1st edition, Porto Alegre (Brasil), Artes e Ofícios Editora, 1992, 144 pp.

PAULO, Isabel, 'The dragon king', *Expresso* (Única), Oeiras, 22nd May, 2004, 9.

'Mourinho leaves Veiga', *Expresso*, Oeiras, 19th January, 2002, 1.
'Paulo Ferreira, newly-made millionaire', *Expresso*, Oeiras, 11th June, 2004, 1.

PARALVAS, Nuno, 'I believe I'm special', *A Bola*, Lisbon, 3rd June, 2004, 2.

PEDROSA, Paulo, 'I'm very proud', *MaisFutebol* (www.maisfutebol.iol.pt) (consulted on 30th March, 2004)
'A spy for 15 years', *MaisFutebol* (www.maisfutebol.iol.pt) (consulted on 30th March, 2004)

PEREIRA, Rui Pedro, 'Mourinho, the conqueror', *Doze*, Lisbon, 19th December, 2003) 8.

PONTES, David; MARQUES, Francisco J.; FARIA, José Pedroso, 'If the president says 'don't leave', I won't leave', *Jornal de Notícias*, Porto, 20th January, 2004, 4.

POWELL, Jeff, 'You don't have to be mad to be a manager. But it does help...', *Daily Mail*, London, 28th May, 2004, 1.

PRATA, Bruno; MOREIRA, José Augusto, 'The Portuguese manager is intelligent and astute', *Público*, Lisbon, 14th July, 2002, 2.

RITA, Pedro, 'Coach finally admitted that he wasn't even going to the final', *Correio da Manhã*, Lisbon, 29th May, 2004, 1.
'The letter from Baidek', *Correio da Manhã*, Lisbon, 30th May, 2004, 1.

ROJO, Luís, 'We're not afraid of Real Madrid', *Marca* (www.marca.com) (consulted on 8th April, 2004).

SILVA, João Carlos, 'Who's Mourinho's new boss?', *24 Horas*, Lisbon, 7th June, 2004, 2.SILVA, Paulo, 'Mourinho's the best!', *24 Horas*, Lisbon, 13th January, 2004, 1.

SILVA, Rita Jordão, 'Chelsea is Mourinho's new challenge', *Público*, Lisbon, 29th May, 2004, 1.
'Mourinho finally at Chelsea', *Público*, Lisbon, 3rd June, 2004, 2.

SILVA, Tiago; PEREIRA, André L., 'Mourinho with Europe at his feet', *Correio da Manhã*, Lisbon, 29th May, 2004, 1.

SOVERAL, Kátia, 'She's the one in charge', *Nova Gente*, Sintra, 29th May, 2004, 3.

TADEIA, António, 'The PREC of FC Porto', *Sábado*, Lisbon, 7th May, 2004, 4.

TAVARES-TELLES, Alexandra, 'The atypical Portuguese man', *Sábado*, Lisbon, 7th May, 2004, 4.

VÁRIOS, *Football Stories*, 1st edition, Lisbon, Relógio D'Água Editores, 2002, 164 pp.

VERÍSSIMO, Luis Fernando, *The endless deprivation of the perfect fullback*, 1st edition, Rio de Janeiro, Editora Objetiva, 1999.